IN DEFENSE OF FREEDOM:

A Conservative Credo

IN DEFENSE OF FREEDOM:

A Conservative Credo

by

FRANK S. MEYER

HENRY REGNERY COMPANY

Chicago 1962

Manufactured in the United States of America

LIBRARY OF CONGRESS CATALOG CARD NUMBER: 62-19389

TO . . .

L. Brent Bozell
William F. Buckley, Jr.
Willmoore Kendall

Companions in battle
Whetstones of the mind

None of whom will by any means agree with much of this book; without whom, however, it could not have been written

CONTENTS

IN DEFENSE OF FREEDOM:

A Conservative Credo

I

FREEDOM AND CONSERVATISM

My intention in writing this book is to vindicate the freedom of the person as the central and primary end of political society. I am also concerned with demonstrating the integral relationship between freedom as a political end and the basic beliefs of contemporary American conservatism.

Liberalism was indeed once, in the last century, the proponent and defender of freedom. But that which is called liberalism today has deserted its heritage of defense of the freedom of the person, to become the peculiarly American form of what in Europe is called democratic socialism. This transformation was the result of a fatal flaw in the philosophical underpinnings of 19th-century liberalism. It stood for individual freedom, but its utilitarian philosophical attitude denied the validity of moral ends firmly based on the constitution of being. Thereby, with this denial of an ultimate sanction for the inviolability of the person, liberalism destroyed the very foundations of its defense of the person as primary in political and social matters.

The complex story of the actual transformation of liberalism—a transformation unfolding out of this profound original defect—is a fascinating chapter in intellectual history. That is not, however, the subject of this book. Although I shall touch upon it from time to time, my concern here is not with the history of liberalism, but with what is today called liberalism—alike by those who are hostile to it and by those who consciously write and act as "liberals." This usage is the only meaning the word retains in common discourse. Therefore, to distinguish contemporary "liberalism" from the liberalism of the 19th century—and in piety towards the 19th-century liberals to whom the freedom of the person was a dear concern—I shall throughout this book refer to what is today called liberalism as "collectivist liberalism."

If, however, 19th-century liberalism by its fundamental philosophical errors gave birth to that form of 20th-century collectivism which passes under the name of liberalism, there was in 19th-century conservatism an inherent flaw of another sort. The conservatives of the last century were sound in their fundamental philosophical position, upholding the objective existence of values based upon the unchanging constitution of being as the criteria for moral thought and action. They staunchly held the line against the assault of utilitarianism, positivism and scientism; but, on another level they failed philosophically, deeply misreading the nature of man. They would not or they could not see the correlative to their fundamental philosophical position: acceptance of the moral authority derived from transcendent criteria of truth and good must be voluntary if it is to have meaning; if it is coerced by human force, it is meaningless. They were willing, if only the right standards were upheld, to accept an authoritarian structure of state and society. They were, at the best, indifferent to freedom in the body politic; at the worst, its enemies.

There are in the contemporary American scene those who take their inspiration from these 19th-century conservative beliefs. Although they do not compose an organized political group (some of them, indeed, in their practical political influence are essentially part of the "liberal" establishment, while others are allied with the American conservative movement), they do hold a common theoretical position. This position is generally described by the term "The New Conservatism." Although that phrase is sometimes also used more broadly, to refer to the whole contemporary American conservative movement, it is in the specific and limited sense that I shall employ it in this book.

The concepts on which the New Conservatives base themselves can be directly traced to 19th-century conservatism and to certain aspects of the thinking of Edmund Burke, who is explicitly recognized by most of them as a major source of their guiding ideas. Their position is characterized by an organic view of society; by a subordination of the individual person to society; and, therefore, by a denial that the freedom of the person is the decisive criterion of a good polity.

This subordination of freedom, this exaltation of the claims of society, differentiates them from the implicit consensus of contemporary American conservatism. That consensus, it is true, does agree with the New Conservatives on the moral obligation of all men to seek and to respect the norms of virtue objectively based upon an eternal order of truth and good; but, in contradistinction to them, it posits as a necessary corollary that the freedom of the person, not the asserted authority of "society," of some "mysterious incorporation of the human race," is primary in political thought and action.

Should the question be raised, by what right do I maintain against the New Conservatives and the other heirs of 19th-century conservatism that the position which I am defending is essentially the consensus of contemporary American conservatism, I point first to the empirical evidence—and on several levels. At the source to which American conservatism inevitably returns—The Declaration of Independence, the Constitution and the debates at the time of its adoption—this simultaneous belief in objectively existing moral value and in the freedom of the individual person was promulgated in uncompromising terms. From that source it irradiates the active present scene of American conservatism. The broadly acknowledged political symbol of American conservatism, Barry Goldwater, and its broadly acknowledged intellectual spokesman, William F. Buckley, Jr., share this twin belief. As M. Stanton Evans, in *Revolt on the Campus*,* has shown in copious quotations from the leaders of the conservative student movement, it is their guiding light. What is true of the young, is also true of the great majority of adult conservatives. A serious examination of the publications of the various groups among conservatives will, I am convinced, prove this contention to the disinterested reader.

The position taken in this book is, I believe, an accurate representation, a crystallization on the theoretical level, of the empirical attitudes of the widespread and developing American conservative move-

* M. Stanton Evans, *Revolt on the Campus* (Chicago: Henry Regnery Co., 1961), pp. 180-185.

ment. But this very combination of freedom and moral authority—which in the ideological history of the European 19th century were the symbols of opposed liberal and conservative forces—has been the target of sharp theoretical attack by collectivist-liberal writers, and even by some conservatives of the 19th-century tradition. We are told that what is not in the tradition of Burke—or of the medieval synthesis—or of Plato—cannot call itself conservatism: anyone who insists upon freedom in the political and economic sphere together with "legitimate" conservative beliefs, is really half liberal, half conservative, a sad case of intellectual schizophrenia. Such criticisms might be answered by simply pointing to actuality, asserting that, whether European intellectual history blesses us or not, this is the way the average contemporary American conservative thinks and feels; or by citing the founding documents of the Republic as authority—the authority of another, an American, intellectual history.

But, in candor, this is not enough. It has to be shown that the two aspects of the position are fundamentally in accord, that they are grounded both in the nature of men and in the very constitution of being. It is my aim to make this demonstration, to vindicate on theoretical grounds the native belief of American conservatives that freedom as a prime criterion in the political and social sphere is not alien to the conservative view of man's nature and destiny; that it arises naturally from conservative assumptions; and that it can be effectively defended only upon the basis of those assumptions.

Therefore, the concern of these pages is with establishing the theoretical soundness of this position. I am not primarily concerned with the details or the limitations of present-day political reality, but rather with developing a conservative criterion for a good society, a good polity. That being my intent, the standard of judgment of political questions here presented is just that: a standard, not a program for immediate achievement. I would add, however, that without something in the nature of an ideal image of what a good society should be, without an end which political action can strive to approximate, there is no basis for judging the rights and wrongs of the practical alternatives that constantly present themselves.

The specific character of the concrete political forms indicated by this criterion for any given society will vary immensely depending on the civilizational development and the experience with free institutions of the nation or culture concerned. In the United States, with our Constitutional tradition and Constitutional experience, a comparatively close approximation to the ideal is possible, despite the attrition of several decades of liberal-collectivist ascendancy. For ours is the most effective effort ever made to articulate in *political* terms the Western understanding of the interrelation of the freedom of the person and the authority of an objective moral order. The other nations of Western civilization—all respecters of the person, but without the rock-bound theory of limited government that inspired the American Founders—hold, in varying degree, the pre-eminence of the person in their tradition; and therefore they approximate, if less closely, to the political ideal here presented. The tradition of the Oriental and Middle Eastern civilizations is still further removed from it; and pre-civilized cultures, such as those of Africa, are at an enormous remove from it.

I realize that such a ranking of nations and cultures, particularly one which places one's own country at the head, will be regarded in the relativist atmosphere of the day as extraordinarily unenlightened and arrogant. Be that as it may, by the criterion I hope to establish, it is the truth; and it is therefore primarily to the United States and secondarily to Western civilization that my analysis has direct relevance.

Furthermore, I should add, lest specious conclusions be drawn from the defense of the freedom of the person, that there is here no advocacy of that equalitarianism which would forbid to men the acquisition of unequal goods, influence or honor, and the right to pass these "inequalities" on to their heirs if they can. The only equality that can be legitimately derived from the premises of the freedom of the person is the equal right of all men to be free from coercion exercised against their life, liberty and property. This is the touchstone of a free society. For the rest, the capabilities of men, specific and inherited, should determine their position, their influence and the respect in which they are held.

Nor does it follow from my thesis that any particular type of political institution is in itself either demanded by, or a guarantee of, development towards a free society. The representative democratic institutions, combined with constitutional guarantees of freedom, which have been the matrix for the development of free societies in the United States, England and some other Western nations, may not be the best political forms for the achievement of an approximation to a good society even in all countries of Western civilization, much less elsewhere.

But, although there is more than one possible form of political institution for the development of a good society, there are also forms which are totally negative to any such development. Nazism, which was inspired by the concept of reducing the person to nothingness before the state, was destroyed in the war of 1939-45; but Communism, its older brother, today dominates a third of the world and advances with messianic zeal and cold scientific strategy towards the domination of the whole world. Consequently, everything projected in this book presupposes the defeat of this monstrous, atavistic attack upon the survival of the very concepts of moral order and individual freedom. If I do not deal with Communism, it is because I am here concerned with the development of ideas within the Western and American tradition. With Communism, which bases itself on a set of values radically hostile in their very foundation to the Western view of man, there is no common ground for theoretical discussion. Determination and force will decide the issue, and our determination and force—which can be expressed only in terms of counter-attack—will depend upon the depth with which we understand, and, understanding, are loyal to, the truths incarnate in Western civilization and the American republic.

To the drawing out and clarification of these truths, this book is dedicated. In that effort, my central endeavor is to validate the individual person as the decisive concern of political action and political theory. The individual person and social institutions are the polar points to which every political philosophy is oriented. And as men's political arrangements reflect their consciousness, it is by the emphasis placed upon one or the other of these poles by the prevalent political philosophy that the characteristics of a political society are established and perpetuated.

It is my general contention that, despite the weight of the tradition of our civilization on the side of the individual person, the predominant intellectual tendency of this century has brought about a deep derangement of the tension between these two poles of human existence, towards the submergence of the person. It is my particular contention that the criticism by the New Conservatives of this prevailing collectivist dogma itself suffers from an inner error of political understanding.

Against both the prevailing mode of thought and the New Conservative criticism, which are, each in its own way, appeals to experience, I propose the claims of reason and the claims of the tradition of reason. I do not assume that reason is the sole possession of a single living generation, or of any man in any generation. I do assume that it is the active quality whereby men (starting with a due respect for the fundamental moral knowledge of ends and values incorporated in tradition) have the power to distinguish what ought to be from what is, the ideal from the dictates of power. Upon these assumptions, I shall attempt to reestablish, in contemporary contexts, principles drawn from the nature of man, and by these principles to criticize both the prevalent collectivist-liberal orthodoxy and the New Conservatism.

Both, I hope to show, share in political matters a common error, which brings them much closer together than the polemics exchanged between them would seem to indicate. Both are radically affected by the derangement of the tension between the person and social institutions necessary to a good society. Both give so high a place to the concept of society that the freedom of the person is reduced to a subordinate position and becomes transformed from a real end into a pious hope—invoked on suitable occasions, but to be achieved as the implicit result of the establishment of the "right" social pattern, not to be striven for directly. Both reduce the person to a secondary being, whose dignity and rights become dependent upon the gift and grace of society or the state.

II

CLEARING GROUND

It is impossible to come to grips with the problem of freedom, and with the interrelated problem of the individual and society, without first clearing some ground. Before the questions themselves can be fruitfully discussed, it is necessary to say something about the way in which we have become accustomed to think and speak of them, about what is now the generally accepted method of political and social thought. That method not only affects fundamental enquiry concerning political and social matters; it also affects our efforts to handle the practical and immediate political situations which press upon us. Our inability to act confidently in the face of upsetting phenomena as divergent as our successive defeats by the Soviet Union in the world arena or the growth of juvenile delinquency, has its roots in a fundamental derangement of our way of thinking about the world. We concentrate upon problems that seem to multiply, hydra-like, rather than upon the principles that bear upon the problems; and this creates the suffocating verbiage of so much contemporary political and social discussion. Like a bevy of old wives congregated about the bedside of a suffering patient, every pundit presses his own nostrum, each directed towards a conspicuous symptom; and, as the chatter arises, it drowns the voice and crazes the mind of anyone attempting to assess the underlying malady which creates the symptoms.

Worse, in the prevailing intellectual atmosphere the very concept of a theoretical enquiry into political and social matters which is based upon a moral or philosophical value-system and developed in terms of the nature of man, is the subject of scorn. By a misleading analogy with physical science—where the objects of study are but objects, without subjectivity, will, conscious self-direction—social theory becomes "the social sciences," political theory becomes "political science," disciplines conceived in slavish imitation of the natural sciences. An entire dimension is exiled from consideration, a dimension which in the natural sciences does not and could not exist: the dimension of the ideal, of the end and direction of action, of what ought to be. But the great tradition of Western thought, which gave form to the political concepts and institutions we have inherited, found in the tension between what ought to be and what is, the beginning and the continuing center of political theory. However different their approach, however different their practical conclusions, this is as true of Dante as of Aquinas, of the Puritan republicans as of the Stuart apologists for the divine right of kings. And, although by the 18th century the corrosive influence of scientism had already begun to eat away at the theoretical foundations of political thought, it remained as true of Adams as of Jefferson, of Calhoun as of Lincoln.

Scientism and the study of politics

Just where and how the other conception, the scientistic conception, the idea that the study of politics is a science in the same sense and with the same methods as the study of natural phenomena, became a central theme and dominant mode of social scholarship: this is a fascinating and depressing study, but one which it would be impossible to develop within the limits of this book. Suffice it to say that today the learned authority upon politics is either the *Realpolitiker*, the political tough guy, who advises those with power how to use it in order to get more power, or the expert on the interview and the statistic, the indefatigable pollster, whose idea of political study is to register the impulses of the uninformed and uninstructed mass. The former considers political thought a "policy science"; the latter, a "behavioral science." But they are in agreement that political science is limited to an analysis of what is, that it has no relationship to moral or philosophical enquiry. This attitude, the influence of which has spread far beyond the confines of scholarship, permeating the outlook of journalist, telecaster and politician, draws its underlying assumptions from the empirical and naturalistic position of Machiavelli and Hobbes. These assumptions have been immensely reinforced in the past hundred years by the prestige the natural sciences and their methods have acquired.

It is here that the prevailing doctrines go astray. The sphere of natural studies contains no element of consciousness with its innate corollary of freedom and moral responsibility. But any study that aspires to throw light upon man must take account of these autonomous aspects of his being. It is possible to study the proton, the meson, the electron, without any consideration of their inner being or of consciousness. Even with non-human life—that intermediate mode of being between the inorganic and the human—there is no way of knowing, language lacking, the degree or level of consciousness. While, by analogy, we may justly attribute a nearer approach to consciousness to animals than to the inorganic world, we still have no forcing knowledge that denies us the right to learn what we can solely by external consideration of their behavior.

A methodology which is richly rewarding when it deals with the "how" of inorganic processes, and which has moderate results insofar as it considers the lower forms of life, can be applied to human beings only by a perversion of the principle of analogy. To do so is deliberately to put blinkers upon our eyes, to refuse to consider the material available to our judgments. The principle of analogy functions validly when, from things we know much about, we derive insights into things about which our information is limited. But to insist that methods which seem valid for the study of fields where consciousness is not involved will bring fruitful results when applied to the study of human beings, who are endowed with consciousness, a study where we are richly provided with direct knowledge of consciousness—this is to transform the principle of analogy into its opposite. It is to move from solid forms to images. Where we have direct knowledge, we do not need analogy. The validity of a method applicable where our information can only be from the outside arises from the fact that it is the best method we have. It is absurd to use such a method in an area where our knowledge from the inside is so rich as to be oftentimes embarrassing.

Any "science" of man which pretends to a fruitful utilization of the methods and techniques of the natural sciences does so and can do so only by ignoring an enormous and decisive aspect of the actuality of men. For men's knowledge of themselves is first of all direct: that which they know of their own consciousness from their own consciousness. To attempt to arrive at an understanding of men indirectly, by an examination of their actions, their "behavior," is to arrive only at knowledge of a truncated mechanical model which resembles man only in externals.

It should be remarked in passing that to reject the validity of the scientific methodology for the study of man is not to deny the usefulness of that methodology in auxiliary studies which are secondarily relevant to the study of man. Even here, however, there is a limitation. Analytical and statistical studies of such problems as population, employment, the geographical distribution of voting trends, can throw light upon the study of man; but they are only reliable under the condition that they measure activities undertaken quite independently of the observer. That is, when a man votes in an election or purchases a commodity on the market, an act has taken place, and it is subject to the same kind of objective observation as the motion of a physical body; but when a sociologist or a "political scientist" asks a set of questions whose sole function is to serve his research, questions in which the man interviewed has no stake, the scientific character is largely vitiated. The results must be judged much as the results achieved by a student of the same process, with no pretensions to the scientific method, would be judged; in both cases the results reflect the understanding and insight of the student of the problem. The quasi-scientific trimmings detract, if anything, from the validity of the findings, for a painful effort of analysis is necessary to discover whatever truths of insight lie behind the statistical findings. In view of the non-independent character of the questions, the answers can reflect little more than the value system and the judgment of those who constructed them.

Scientific method, in a word, is valid for the study of man only when it is possible to study unaffected behavior objectively; and its value is limited and auxiliary, because the conclusions achieved will not be knowledge *of* men, but simply knowledge of some aspects of their behavior. Only when it is assumed, in sycophantic imitation of the natural sciences, that there is no valid knowledge except knowledge of that which can be objectively observed, manipulated, and measured, can the study of behavior be substituted for the study of man and glorified as the only possible form of the study of man.

The appeal from Marx to Freud

In recent years, it is true, the poverty of the results achieved by the accepted methods has impelled a turn among social scientists from total concentration upon behavioral social processes towards grudging consideration of the possible significance of individuality.

But so divorced have contemporary scholars become from the broader philosophical tradition, and so concerned are the social scientists lest they move outside the methodology of the natural sciences. that the individual person with whom they pretend to deal turns out to have a curious identity with the robot of the social behaviorism they began by criticizing. Between the views of W. H. MacDougall or George H. Mead and those of Clyde Kluckhohn or Margaret Mead, the essential difference is very slight indeed.

The appeal now is to Freud, but not to the dynamic Freud who, when deterministic scientism had deprived man of soul and free will, at least gave him back an autonomous biological constitution and a free "id." Rather it takes from psychoanalysis—preferably from the watered-down socialized neo-Freudianism of Sullivan, Fromm, and Horney—a set of descriptive terms with which it proceeds to construct its "models" of man, "models" distinguished from the earlier models of the social determinists only as Detroit generally distinguishes this year's model from last year's—by a somewhat different and, for the moment, more fashionable placing of the chrome.

Looking back upon the earlier trend of sociology with its tremendous debt to Marx, and contrasting it with what they fondly describe as a new "turn," from emphasis upon "man in general [to] the individual person," two eminent sociologists of the new dispensation write: "If Marx stratified man, then Freud individualized him. Marxian theory focused our attention upon the coercive role of culture and stressed the process of social change. Freudian theory illuminated the behavior of individual personalities subjected to this cultural patterning and stressed the process of social adjustment."*

This would seem to say that Marx (and with him the main 20th-century trend in the social sciences) concentrated our attention upon society's role as omnipotent creator and controller of the person, while Freud concentrated it upon the way in which the person is created and controlled by society. This interpretation of Freud is no more a charter for the individual than are the theories of Marx. And indeed the writers go on to say, in an incredible contradiction which shows how alien to their minds is the concept of freedom: ". . . Freud set man free . . . Freud set man afloat in an interpersonal universe by making untenable [the] historic conception of man as a rational, volitional, autonomous individual."**

The autonomy of man

Neither to the older nor to the newer forms of the scientistic methodology will this book make any concessions. Its fundamental premise *is* the "historic con-

* Ernest R. Hilgard and Daniel Lerner, "The Person: Subject and Object of Science and Policy," in *The Policy Sciences*, edited by Daniel Lerner and Harold D. Lasswell (Stanford University Press, 1951), p. 17.

** *The Policy Sciences*, p. 17.

ception of man as a rational, volitional, autonomous individual," as a free being who lives between good and evil, beauty and ugliness, truth and error, and fulfills his destiny in the choices he makes.

This power to make choices, this innate freedom lies at the center of the drama of human existence. It is given immediately to every man's consciousness as a primary datum, along with his awareness of "the other," the externally determined, the objective world. Indeed, in mutual opposition, the self and "the other," the subjective and the objective, define each other and together exhaustively constitute the primitive content of consciousness. No objective methodology, however strict, can disprove the existence of the autonomous self and validate determinism, as no intuitive outlook, based upon the subjective, can disprove the existence of the external world and validate solipsism.

The "interpersonal" universe, like the universe of the behaviorists or the cultural relativists, rests upon data derived from apprehension of the external world. But that apprehension is no stronger than its twin apprehension: apprehension of the subjective, of the autonomy of the person. Therefore, no system built upon the one apprehension can logically deny the validity of the other without denying its own validity. To the degree that a fundamental premise systematically neglects either side of the tension between self and non-self, which is the only ground from which human thought can in reality proceed, it must perforce limp one-leggedly behind the full capacities of human understanding.

Primary assumptions

The apprehension of man as of such a nature that innate freedom is of the essence of his being, is the central axiom upon which this critique of political thought is founded. It further assumes that the primary mode of achieving understanding in the study of man, more particularly in moral and political enquiry, is the use of reason operating within and upon tradition, reason deriving extended conclusions from simple apprehensions of the nature of man. Man as he exists, a complex whole, is the starting point. The conclusions are the principles which define the social and political conditions under which he can best fulfill his innate destiny.

They are, indeed, ideal principles and must be adapted in the light of the material situation and the demands of conflicting interests. They will need to be made concrete in different ways under different circumstances. But, although the ideal conclusions of political theory are not programmatic directives for detailed political action, this in no way negates the role and necessity of political theory. To bring about an approximation in actuality to an ideal set of limiting conditions is, or should be, the function of the art of politics, not the function of political theory. To think otherwise would be Utopian, to conceive once more of men as manipulable particles subject to the forming activity of the social engineer. The art of politics at its best is guided by fundamental principle, but operates by judgment, by prudence. Both are necessary; without the guiding principles of political theory, based in turn upon fundamental philosophical considerations, the practical art of politics is without direction and soon becomes an exercise in expediency for expediency's sake.

III

WHY FREEDOM?

To the primary proposition that innate freedom is an essential aspect of man's being, I join another proposition of a more specifically political character: that social and political organization, however important as a condition of existence, is, like oxygen or water, a condition, not the end, of the life of the individual person. At the best, proper social and political circumstances, like a rich and well-tilled seed-bed, can provide felicitous circumstances in which a man may work out his fortune or misfortune, his good or ill. At the worst, they may cramp the field of his existence to a compass scarcely recognizable as human, although even then they cannot destroy the self-determination of his inner spiritual life. But, at best or worse, the social and political situation remains a situation more or less conducive to the worthy consummation of each man's drama, not a determining factor of it.

In one period of happier circumstance, Oliver Goldsmith and Dr. Johnson wrote:

> How small, of all that human hearts endure,
> That part which kings or laws can cause or cure!

The joint development of modern science and totalitarianism has increased the evil that state power can cause, but there is still a very small part of that which "human hearts endure" that the state can alleviate. So far as the increased power of the state to bring evil to the individual is concerned, that power is directly proportional to the pretences the state makes to control men's lives for good. To the degree that the political theory upon which the state is founded regards political and social institutions not simply as a condition of human existence, but as the determining cause of the well-being of men, the more it becomes an active source of ill-being. This much one can concede as a 20th-century gloss on the 18-century couplet: the state can cause greater harm than then, but cure no more.

Society not a real entity

That which is not a determining cause but merely a condition, cannot be considered independently as a true end; it must be considered in subordination to that of which it is a condition. Society and the state were made for individual men, not men for them. This was once a truism in America and through much of the West; but in the past few decades all the prospering political ideologies—Communism and Nazism, socialism, the milder theories of the welfare state—have founded themselves upon the opposite axiom, that individual men are secondary to society.

True, all these societal views proclaim—Communists no less than the social worker servitors of the welfare state—that they are directed towards the welfare of men, or at least towards the greatest welfare of the greatest number of men. But in all of them, the ground of the value judgments upon which every crucial decision is based is the abstract construct, society. None of them ever takes the person—not in mass, not in grouped "minorities," but in his single majesty, one individual—as the criterion by which the validity of political and social decisions is to be judged.

It is true, of course, that there would be no political or social institutions, nor any meaning to political enquiry, if men lived as single isolated individuals. To insist, as I do, that the individual is the criterion by which institutions and political theories should be judged is not to deny the immediate and obvious meaning of the phrase, "man is a social animal," that is, that each man has a multifarious set of relationships with other men.

The error arises when from this simple truism the conclusion is drawn that the set of relationships between men itself constitutes a real entity—an organism, as it were—called "society," with a life and with moral duties and rights of its own. This hypostatization of the sum of relations between men, this calling into being of an organism as the value-center of political theory, is the essential note of the doctrines which underlie and inspire every powerful political movement of the 20th century and all the effective transformations of political institutions which have taken place in the 20th century.

By the nature of the case, if society is an organism, the men who make it up can be no more than cells in the body of society; and society, not they, becomes the criterion by which moral and political matters are judged. It is in society, not in the individuals who make it up, that right inheres; and whatever "rights" individual men may be allowed are pseudo-rights, granted and revocable by society. The moral claims of the person are in effect reduced to nothingness.

The myth of society

This, in one form or another, is the prevailing political doctrine of our time, a doctrine so widely and uncritically held that it has almost ceased to be doctrine and become a myth, largely below the level of conscious discourse. It is not thought about, but is itself constitutive of the forms of thought on political and social matters; and it establishes an atmosphere in which neither in political action nor in political thought are first principles considered—nor is the fundamental societarian premise itself critically assessed. This state of affairs is reflected almost universally—no less in the pronouncements of Presidents, the judgments of the highest courts and the deliberations of the Congress than in university lectures, learned journals and scholarly studies.

It takes what is probably its most extreme form in the writings of the most influential schools of contemporary sociology.* Benjamin Schwartz, a sociologist himself, writing of certain trends among his colleagues, has epitomized what is in fact characteristic not only of most sociologists, but of most social scientists of all specialties. He attacks

a natural tendency . . . to reduce the "isolated individual" to as rudimentary a model as possible, thus

* The indirect influence of this discipline upon political thought has been great for many decades. But if the example of the Supreme Court decision in the 1954 school-segregation case, *Brown v. Board of Education*, is to be a precedent, that influence is now to become directly legislative; for in this case the Court in its decision relied primarily not upon principles of law, natural or positive, not upon Constitutional prescription or Congressional statute, but directly upon the theories of contemporary sociologists.

allowing full scope to social structure as a determining factor. Were it not for the annoying fact that the individual assumes the form of a biological organism, they might be able to claim him entirely.*

Or, as B. F. Skinner, Professor of Psychology at Harvard University, puts it:

. . . as the use of science increases, we are forced to accept the theoretical structure with which science represents its facts. . . . Every discovery of an event which has a part in shaping a man's behavior seems to leave so much the less to be credited to the man himself; and as such explanations become more and more comprehensive, the contributions which may be claimed by the individual himself appear to approach zero. Man's vaunted creative powers, his original accomplishments in art, science and morals, his capacity to choose and our right to hold him responsible for the consequences of his choice—none of these is conspicuous in this new self-portrait.

Man, we once believed, was free to express himself in art, music and literature, to inquire into nature, to seek salvation in his own way. He could initiate action and make spontaneous and capricious changes of course. Under the most extreme duress some sort of choice remained to him. He could resist any effort to control him, though it might cost him his life. But science insists that action is initiated by forces im-

* Benjamin Schwartz, "The Socio-Historic Approach," *World Politics*, October, 1955, p. 134.

pinging upon the individual, and that caprice is only another name for behavior for which we have not yet found a cause.*

. . . science ultimately explains behavior in terms of "causes" or conditions which lie beyond the individual himself. As more and more causal relations are demonstrated, a practical corollary becomes difficult to resist: it should be possible to *produce* behavior according to plan simply by arranging the proper conditions.**

In turning to the external conditions which shape and maintain the behavior of men, while questioning the reality of inner qualities and faculties to which human achievements were once [!] attributed, we turn from the ill-defined and remote to the observable and manipulable.†

The social engineering concept of the control of men for purposes "scientifically" adumbrated and the collectivist concept which devalues men's status as individual persons for the glorification of society and state are inherently interrelated. And, curiously, considering the scientific and "value-free" predilections of those who posit these associated concepts, a third element always seems necessary to complete the symbiotic conceptual environment: "human welfare."

* B. F. Skinner, "Freedom and the Control of Men," *The American Scholar*, Winter, 1955-56, pp. 52-53.

** p. 47.

† pp. 64-65.

This it is which even so hard-boiled a proponent of "cultural engineering" (his own term) as Professor Skinner presents as the end of his endeavors. But this, which one would think, being an end, should be the most firmly based of his concepts, is entirely vague —a mere pious decoration without content. The improvements in man towards which his engineering would be devoted relate to nothing in particular. What they are founded on "are not value judgments —they are guesses. To confuse and delay the improvement of cultural practices by quibbling about the word *improve* is itself not a useful practice."*

As with so many of his *compères*, academic and political, Professor Skinner's thought, skipping lightly over the undefined—and, it would appear, purely verbal—end of welfare, lands heavily upon the vital element of his conceptual apparatus: power. The words in which his dominant ideas are expressed are all derived from the rhetoric of power. His vision is one of "improving," "transforming," "controlling," "manipulating"—always by some unspecified élite (scientists, of course) operating upon other human beings.

Human beings considered as the objects of operations are no more nor less than . . . objects. Kant's imperative is reversed. Our humanitarians of the welfare

---

* pp. 50-51.

society take as their maxim: treat no person as an end, but only as a means to arrive at a general good.

Of course, it is not often that one finds so theoretically developed and uncompromising a statement as Professor Skinner's of the underlying beliefs upon which the liberal-collectivist *Weltanschauung* is based. This is for two reasons. In the first place, the positivist attitude and the admiration for the "value-free" methods of the natural sciences, which characterize the intellectual atmosphere, tend against the systematic statement of principle. The devaluation of the individual and the glorification of the collective is arrived at negatively: theoretically by a relativist criticism of the traditional value system and practically in the course of a variegated series of separate and detached social, economic and political projects. The New Deal itself, which was decisive in the triumph of liberal collectivism in the United States, proceeded without any observable over-all theory, by just such a series of projects. If one looks for general characteristics binding together these separate projects, one will find (apart from the fact that they all led towards an increase in the power of the state and a decrease in that of the person) only a sentimental *mystique* of welfare and a constant insistence upon the virtue of the pragmatic as over against the traditional ("horse-and-buggy economy for an automobile age").

In the second place, there still remains in the minds

of the bearers of the contemporary relativist ideology a residue of absolute moral value, the heritage of their birth and upbringing in Western civilization, which is solidly based upon absolute value. The most relativist, the most instrumentalist of those who preach the mutability of morality would personally long hesitate before violating the moral principles he learned from the parents of his childhood or the church of his youth.* And similarly, when the blatant results of a naturalism free of the trammels of transcendent value are expressed socially in the logical rigor of totalitarian systems (which kill by wholesale for the sake of the Plan) or in juvenile delinquent gangs (which kill by retail for the sake of a thrill), they reject with horror phenomena which are entirely consistent with their philosophical position.** They are living on moral capital, their actions and attitudes modified by personal habits acquired under the tutelage of philosophies very different from theirs.

---

* So at least for the generation now dominant. What will be the case with *their* children, who have never had these experiences, is fearsome to contemplate.

** I do not say the only type of phenomena consistent with it. Beneficent impulses leading spontaneously to beneficent acts would be just as consistent with it. The point is that neither bad impulses nor good ones, bad acts nor good ones, are inconsistent with a relativist philosophy, since there is no criterion of bad or good by which they can be judged—only an endless series of changes upon the theme of undirected efficacy: useful or non-useful; instrumental or non-meaningful—that is, not instrumental; socially directed or "destructive."

The liberal-collectivist dogma

Nevertheless, however untheoretically stated, however inconsistently reflected in the actions of individuals in specific situations, a broadly consistent and delimitable body of dogma pervades the decisive and articulate sections of our society, shaping the minds of those who form opinion and create the conditions within which public decisions are made.

Philosophically, this body of dogma is relativist, pragmatic, positivist, scornful of absolute criteria, of all strictly theoretical thought, of all enquiry not amenable to the methods of the natural sciences.

Socially, it assumes the existence of an organism, "society," as the being to which, and to the good of which, all moral (and by the same token, political) problems finally refer. Sometimes this principle is modified, but never by intrinsic reference to the individual person, only (when the totalitarian implications of total reference to "society" loom too large) by reference to collectivist images of specialized groups of individuals: "minorities," "the underprivileged," "the élite," "scientists," "gifted children," "backward children," "labor." Concern is never for, there is no moral reference to, a man who is a Negro, a poor man, a rich man, a well-born man, an able man, a biologist, a child, a carpenter.

Politically, it attributes virtue in strict proportionality to power. Actions are best, and best performed, when the state performs them; and within the governmental structure, best when the act of the Federal government rather than of the several states; and within the Federal government, best when the action of the executive rather than of the legislature. And if it cannot be the act of government, better that it be the act of an organization than that of an individual, better that of a large organization than that of a small one. Virtue resides infinitely more in the United Steel Workers of America than in any individual steel worker; more in the NAACP, than in any individual colored person; more in the AAUP, than in any university professor, however distinguished.

Economically, it takes for granted that the several energies of men expressed through the functioning of a free-market economy can lead only to disaster (although it was with the growth of that system that the great leap in human productivity of the last 150 years occurred). Considering centralized direction and regulation the desideratum of economic systems, it either looks towards state ownership of all productive facilities, in a Marxist or quasi-Marxist manner, or, in a Keynesian manner, it demands that in a "mixed economy" the state control all the decisive sectors of the economy and receive a lion's share, through taxation, of the product. In either case it insists that only "socially desirable" production shall be encouraged; and that the decision as to what is "socially desirable" shall be made not by individual consumers through the market, but by bureaucrats and social workers through the power of regulation and taxation.

Emotionally, it prefers psychoanalysis to the dark night of the soul, "adjustment" to achievement, security to freedom. It preaches "the end of ideology," admires experts and fears prophets, fears above all commitment to value transcending the fact.

These, broadly stated, are the tenets of the prevailing liberal-collectivist orthodoxy.

The New Conservatism

It is in challenge to this orthodoxy that the movement of thought which has come to be called the New Conservatism presents itself. The New Conservatism is a palpable body of opinion, but a body of opinion which it is somewhat difficult to delimit. It has no organization; it has issued no manifesto; some of its leading spokesmen, indeed, never use the phrase "New Conservatism," but prefer to speak of "a conservatism of reflection" or "enlightened conservatism." But it is nonetheless a coherent and reasonably specific set of political theories projected by an intellectually influential group. It is recognized as a definite school of thought not only by other political theorists and in academic and critical circles generally, but also in the wider world.

Peter Viereck, Clinton Rossiter, and Russell Kirk are its most widely recognized interpreters; and, of these, Kirk is undoubtedly the most influential. It is to him that I shall most frequently refer in my discussion of the New Conservatism, as the most typical and authoritative champion of its position and its mode of thought.*

These are the best known of those who have worked out the New Conservative position; but there are a considerable number of other scholars whose contributions to this body of thought are of great importance, and I shall have occasion from time to time to refer to them. A list, by no means exhaustive, of the more distinguished of these might include such names as Robert A. Nisbet, John H. Hallowell, the late Gordon K. Chalmers, Thomas I. Cook, and Peter Drucker. One might go on indefinitely, particularly if account were taken of those who exist in the vague penumbra of the New Conservative influence. Publicists like Walter Lippmann reflect some of its ideas. Even active participants in the liberal-collectivist political world, like George Kennan, Reinhold Niebuhr,

---

* I refer to Mr. Kirk's fundamental position, as developed in his major works, *The Conservative Mind* and *A Program for Conservatives*, and also in his writings up to very recently. In the last year or two, however, in a number of his contributions to periodicals, there has been observable some weakening in his intransigeant New Conservative position and some sign of a greater sympathy with the position of the American conservative consensus on individual freedom.

and August Heckscher, frequently use a rhetoric, and sometimes concepts, not unlike those of the New Conservatism.

Just as it shades off on the one hand into the platitudes of editorialists for "modern Republicanism," or the rhetoric of sated New Dealers in a mood to consolidate the Roosevelt revolution and sanctify it with a conservative aura, so on the other hand it sometimes is confused with the very different approaches of such conservative analysts of political philosophy as Eric Voegelin, Leo Strauss, and Willmoore Kendall, or of such critics as Richard Weaver and Frederick Wilhelmsen.* But these latter scholars are distinguished from the New Conservatives by the much greater intransigeance of their criticism of collectivist liberalism and by a radically different philosophical attitude. The high value they place upon the faculty of reason for the establishing of conservative principles separates them sharply from the New Conservatives, who insist upon the undifferentiated virtue of tradi-

---

* Likewise, I do not consider among the New Conservatives those English or Continental writers who are sometimes grouped with them: such men as Michael Oakeshott, the late Lord Percy of Newcastle, Bertrand de Jouvenel, Erik von Kuehnelt-Leddihn, as well as Wilhelm Roepke and his "neo-liberal" associates. The European situation differs so sharply from the American that even those like Michael Oakeshott, who are closest to the attitudes of the New Conservatism, represent a rather different phenomenon; and most of these men are even further removed from its position.

tion, not merely as guide and governor of reason, but over against reason.

The place of principle

This attitude towards reason is the characteristic methodological sign of the New Conservatism, which elevates the historical process, the venerable, the established, the prescriptive, as the touchstone of the good and the true. While the process of history is seen as Providential dispensation, and the intellectual appeal is to the tradition of Burke, the mode of thought is that which was brought to its highest perfection by Hegel; and as a mode of thought, it suffers from the same innate difficulties as does the Hegelian.

These men are not statesmen like Burke; the prudential choice between immediate practical alternatives, which is the proper task of the statesman, leads in the scholar, the political theorist, to a theoretical impasse. It is one thing for the impassioned author of *Reflections on the Revolution in France*, the defender of a powerful, a solid constitution, not seriously challenged at home, to depend upon the traditional existence of that constitution as its sole sanction and warrant. But the New Conservatives are concerned with the salvation of their civilization and their country from positivist and liberal-collectivist doctrines which are already far advanced in authority over the minds and hearts of men. The values they purport to defend *are* seriously challenged at home. To make *their* sole sanction prescription, to condemn the effort to judge society by theoretical standards, to disparage the exercise of the faculty of reason in that effort as "abstract speculation" and "defecated rationality,"—this is to put themselves at the mercy of the very forces they are proposing to combat. It leaves them in a dilemma from which there is no logical escape.

Either the whole historical and social situation in which they find themselves, including the development of collectivism, statism, and intellectual anarchy, is Providential, and all prescriptive attitudes, including the orthodox collectivist attitudes of the day, are right and true: in which case there is no justification for their stand as an opposition. Or, there is a higher sanction than prescription and tradition; there are standards of truth and good by which men must make their ultimate judgment of ideas and institutions; in which case, reason, operating against the background of tradition, is the faculty upon which they must depend in making that judgment.

It is the same dilemma as that created by the Hegelian dictum: all that is real is rational. Nor is Hegel's own mystical escape from the impasse available to the New Conservatives, who do not accept his dialectic. Within the limits of the complex and powerful myth which he created, he could confute the obvious—that much that exists is irrational—by denying the reality of phenomena which contradicted his thesis, by pairing with "all that is real is rational," the parallel statement, "all that is rational is real."

Such refinements do not exist in the Burkean heritage. Although the particular form that Burke's thinking took at the historical moment in which he found himself is undoubtedly in the direct ancestry of Hegel's system,* Burke himself was too much the hard-headed Englishman to have sought such a solution, had he faced the sort of problem his *soi-disant* heirs do. He would have been more likely, I believe, in conditions such as ours today to have drawn upon the other, the submerged side of his thinking, his fundamental belief in natural rights and in reason as their interpreter. And this, I think, he also would have done, had he lived in 1688, at the time of the Revolution whose established results he celebrates prescriptively a hundred years later. In his struggle against the French Revolution and its perversion of the doctrine of natural rights, this aspect of his thinking fell into

* "Prescription cannot be the sole authority for a constitution, and therefore recourse to rights anterior to the constitution, i.e., to natural rights, cannot be superfluous unless prescription by itself is a sufficient guaranty of goodness. Transcendent standards can be dispensed with if the standard is inherent in the process; 'the actual and the present is the rational.' What could appear as a return to the primeval equation of the good with the ancestral is, in fact, a preparation for Hegel." Leo Strauss, *Natural Right and History* (Chicago: University of Chicago Press, 1953), p. 319.

desuetude, but it was always there in the background, giving foundation and firmness to his exercise of prudence and expedience.

Our contemporary Burkeans will, of course, have none of the Hegelian mysticism; and they continue to reject the appeal to principle, even in the terms that Burke might have allowed. The only way out of their impasse is the way they take: to deny that it is an impasse, to insist that the great tradition of the West is still dominant in the West. Despite the evidence of their senses, they brush away the prevailing power of the outlook which is in fact dominant in the schools and universities, dominant in the mass-communications industries, dominant in the bureaucracy of government, dominant in every decisive position in the land.

By denying the immense and tragic impact of the revolution in accepted ways of thought that the past half-century—and particularly the years since 1932—has brought forth, they are saved the need for recourse to principle. The wave of the present which seems to be carrying us towards the questionable alternative of a Brave New World or a 1984, they can pooh-pooh as nothing but evanescent ripples, froth created by a few already discredited "defecated intellectuals." All that is necessary to return to health and sanity, they insist, is to ignore these temporary and feeble ripples of opinion.

Every twist of the radio or television dial, every turn of the pages of the daily paper or of our magazines, high-brow, low-brow, or middle brow, every act of our governors reflects those opinions. This is a new "tradition," which, if unchallenged, will eclipse the long tradition of America and the West, less crudely than Orwell's Ministry of Truth destroyed history in the interests of a ruling oligarchy, but as effectively. Between the claims of a newly imposed prescriptive outlook, heir to two hundred years or more of "enlightened" nay-saying to the possibility of truth, and the claims of the older tradition upon which this Republic was founded, the tradition of Greece and Israel and Christianity, only a choice based upon principle can decide. But to the patent facts of contemporary history, they turn their blind eye.

To recognize that there is a need to distinguish between traditions, to choose between the good and the evil in tradition, requires recognition of the preeminent role (not, lest I be misunderstood, the sole role) of reason in distinguishing among the possibilities which have been open to men since the serpent tempted Eve, and Adam ate of the Tree of the Knowledge of Good and Evil. But this is exactly what the New Conservatives refuse to recognize. The refusal to recognize the role of reason, the refusal to acknowledge that, in the immense flow of tradition, there are in fact diverse elements that must be distinguished on a principled basis and considered in their relationship to present realities, is a central attribute of New Conservative thought.

It is this which separates the New Conservatism from the conservatism of principle that rejects Burke and the Burkean approach, since being "grounded in the nature of a situation rather than in the nature of things, its opposition will not be a dialectically opposed opposition . . ."* The proponents of the conservatism of principle see that the coherent and comprehensive character of the ascendant thought of the day is not to be countered by anything less than an opposition of principle, which digs to the theoretical roots, indulging necessarily in what Burke called "metaphysical distinctions"—adding, "I hate the very sound of them."**

Burke, like his followers, raised the virtue of prudence, the faculty that adapts general principles to concrete circumstances, to an independent and decisive place. There, instead of complementing the role of reason in political thought, it reduces political

---

* Richard M. Weaver, *The Ethics of Rhetoric* (Chicago: Henry Regnery Co., 1953), p. 83.

** *The Works of Edmund Burke*, Vol. I (London: George Bell & Sons, 1902 [Bohn edition]), p. 432.

thought to what our contemporary sociologists would call "situational analysis." It is for this reason that Richard Weaver says:

> . . . Burke should not be taken as prophet by the political conservatives. True, he has left many wonderful materials which they should assimilate. His insights into human nature are quite solid propositions to build with, and his eloquence is a lesson for all time in the effective power of energy and imagery. Yet these are the auxiliary rhetorical appeals. For the rhetorical appeal on which it will stake its life, a cause must have some primary source of argument which will not be embarrassed by abstractions or even by absolutes—the general ideas mentioned by Tocqueville. Burke was magnificent at embellishment, but of clear rational principle he had a mortal distrust. It could almost be said that he raised "muddling through" to the height of a science, though in actuality it can never be a science. In the most critical undertaking of all, the choice of one's source of argument, it would be blindness to take him as mentor.*

The dread of definition, of distinction, of clear rational principle is characteristic of the New Conservatism. Telling though many of its criticisms are —of the aridity, the "other-directedness," the materialism of the contemporary scene—the New Conservatism is self-disarmed in its chosen task. Rejection

* *The Ethics of Rhetoric*, pp. 83-84.

of the weapon of reason forecloses the possibility of a consistent and cogent attack upon the liberal-collectivist philosophy which lies behind those conditions.

The concept of Providence, upon which New Conservative political thought depends, is undoubtedly an essential part of the Western and Christian tradition. But in this tradition the concept of God's Providence as immanent, as operating within the flow of historical experience, is always in tension with the concept of God as transcendent, as the Ground and Standard of truth and good. When, however, the concept of Providence appears as a determining factor in the political theory of the New Conservatism—most explicitly in the writings of Russell Kirk, but implicitly in all the arguments of the New Conservatives—it is overwhelmingly immanentist. That is to say, it assumes that the Divine Will is expressed *in* the march of events, and therefore that it is *to* the march of events, to history and the tradition embodied in history, that we must look for the ground and standard of truth and good.

Ultimately, no doubt, there is a difference between this concept of history as the expression of the immanent working of Providence and the positivist identification of what ought to be with what is, of truth with experience. But methodologically, in the field of political theory, they are similar. Both reject the necessity of a disciplined philosophical establishment of criteria by which political societies should be judged. Both deny that such an enquiry is necessarily prior to all prudential judging of actuality. Both, that is, elevate the practical act of judgment — which should be based on theory and principle—to the be-all and end-all of political thought.

It is true that abstract theoretical principles cannot be applied without consideration of circumstances, of the possibilities which in fact exist at a given time. That, however, does not mean that prudence can successfully function without the guidance of reason. It does not mean that because concrete circumstances *affect* the application of principle, they therefore *replace* principle and become the sole determinant of political theory. Action based upon political theory thus empirically conceived becomes the sheerest expediency, with no end or purpose but to maneuver upon the wave of the present. The rejection of reason and principle as decisive factors leaves no other course open.

The necessity of freedom

As a result, New Conservative thought can give no more substantial meaning to freedom than can the positivism against which it arrays itself. There is a dichotomy between historical experience as a theater in which men work out their drama and the transcendent standard of truth and good from which that drama takes meaning. If this dichotomy is not recognized, then there can be no choice, and with no choice, no freedom. Either men must go willingly in the direction in which history moves, or they will go unwillingly. *Ducunt Fata volentem, nolentem trahunt.* Only if there exists a real choice between right and wrong, truth and error, a choice which can be made irrespective of the direction in which history and impersonal Fate move, do men possess true freedom.

This is the meaning of the lines from the inscription above the Gate of Hell in Dante's *Inferno*, lines which ever remain a stumbling block to anyone, atheist or theist, who will not see that the glory of man's being is that he is free to choose good or evil, truth or error:

> Giustizia mosse il mio alto Fattore;
> fecemi la divina Potestate,
> la somma Sapienza *e il primo Amore*

> Justice moved my great Maker; the Power of God,
> His supreme Wisdom and *His primal Love* created me.

The words I have emphasized are the boggling point: primal Love. And they are made more scandalous still if one attempts to illuminate them in the light of a sentence from a contemporary Christian apologist (I have forgotten from whom, but it was probably Charles Williams or C. S. Lewis): "Hell is God's last gift to man." But freedom can exist at no lesser price than the danger of damnation; and if freedom is indeed the essence of man's being, that which distinguishes him from the beasts, he must be free to choose his worst as well as his best end. Unless he can choose his worst, he cannot *choose* his best.

No philosophical position that looks to the flow of existence as the sole standard of judgment has any place for true choice. It does not, for this purpose, matter whether the flow of existence is regarded as expressing Divine Providence or the dialectical play of the Absolute, or is thought of as self-contained, non-teleological, a simple positivist assemblage of data. The decisive point is that for any of these positions, freedom can only mean some variation on the Hegelian "freedom is the recognition of necessity." The content of necessity may be variously conceived; it may be regarded as the immutable objective development of the ideal (Hegel), or as an immanent Providence (Kirk), or simply as that which is (the positivists). But, however "necessity" is regarded, to define freedom as recognition, understanding, acceptance of it, is to make the concept of freedom meaningless. Such "recognition" is not a moral act, an act of choice, an act of the will; it has nothing to do with choice. All that is involved is sufficient understanding to know in what direction things are moving, which way one will be dragged if one does not willingly go along. For the human person this is not freedom; it is external determination of his life. It is a heads-I-win, tails-you-lose proposition. It reduces him from a person whose understanding enlightens his will by bringing existence before the bar of essential principle, to a somewhat exalted I.B.M. machine, which registers what experiential existence feeds into it and makes prudential judgments accordingly.

The person, the free human being, is one who can maneuver on the wave of the present if he finds it good, but who will set his face resolutely against it if he finds it bad—even though in a material and practical sense this latter course means that he will be dashed to pieces on the rocks. There are times when the choice which is the expression of freedom as it affects immediate action may be reduced to just so simple an alternative. But even then, morally and spiritually (and in the long run of history, often practically) that choice is a real choice.

The calculating machine can only decide unerringly for security, for survival, for acquiescence in what is and what is becoming. The human being can say quite simply—and literally: to Hell with it; it is wrong and it is false, and in my inner being I will have no part of it, whatever may be forced upon me physically. Fitzjames Stephen, his deeper insights, as they sometimes did, breaking through the utilitarian structure of his thought, has put the matter with all succinctness: "The waters are out and no human force can turn them back, but I do not see why as we go with the stream we need sing Hallelujah to the river god."* Sometimes the choice available may be no more than this, to refuse to acquiesce. But such a choice is impossible when reason and principle are scorned, when virtue is reduced to prudence, when the search for truth is castigated as abstract speculation.

In less extreme situations also, freedom in its true sense, the exercise of choice, is ruled out by the position the New Conservatives maintain. To be sure, they talk a good deal about freedom, as do also the liberal-collectivist positivists and the Hegelians; but when they speak of freedom they mean doing what has to be done or what ought to be done. Freedom never means to them the only thing it can mean if it is not to be reduced to necessity or duty. But necessity and duty are perfectly adequate concepts and there is

* James Fitzjames Stephen, *Liberty, Equality, Fraternity* (London: Smith, Elder, and Co., 1873), p. 242.

no reason why they cannot carry the weight of their own meaning. Freedom means freedom: not necessity, but choice; not responsibility, but the choice between responsibility and irresponsibility; not duty, but the choice between accepting and rejecting duty; not virtue, but the choice between virtue and vice.

Freedom and its uses

I am not defending blind and frivolous action, irresponsibility, immorality or amorality. I believe there are absolute truths and absolute values towards which men should direct themselves. I am only insisting that freedom cannot be defined in terms of the ends that a free person ought to choose, that freedom, which is the power to choose, cannot be identified with what is chosen.

This may seem so self-evident as hardly to need argument; but, unfortunately, it always has and it continues to. As for Hegel "freedom is the recognition of necessity," and for the rationalist "freedom is freedom to do the right," and for the scientificist freedom is an illusion cloaking the materially determined character of all human responses, so in a parallel manner the New Conservative continuously and strenuously reduces freedom to meaninglessness.

John Hallowell, for example, writes:

> A new social philosophy . . . will recognize that freedom is directed toward ends more ultimate than freedom itself. For freedom is not an end in itself . . . but an essential means to the development of moral and spiritual perfection. *And it loses its meaning and degenerates into license if it is not directed toward that end.** [My emphasis, F.S.M.]

His argument is typical of the attitude of the New Conservatism towards the concept of freedom. To the implied questions, what is freedom? and, is it valuable?, he replies with an elaborate begging of the questions. What he says amounts to this: (1) Freedom which is not utilized to achieve right ends "is an empty kind of freedom." (2) Since it is only a means to a given set of ends, if it is used for any other purpose than the achievement of those ends, it becomes something else, something which is neither defined nor characterized, except by being given an ugly name, "license."

The difficulty is that the rose by the ugly name smells just as sweet. Freedom-license remains the unrestrained power to choose — whether the choice made is good or bad. Of the nature of freedom the argument tells us nothing, for it splits the very concept it is presumably defining and judging, defining

---

* John H. Hallowell, *The Moral Foundation of Democracy* (Chicago: University of Chicago Press, 1954), p. 87.

it differently and judging it differently not in accordance with any difference of essence, but solely in accordance with the accidental and external question of how it is used. A rose is not a stink-weed because it gives some people rose fever. In thus refusing to consider freedom as a unitary concept, Mr. Hallowell avoids the difficult problem of the relation of freedom to the end of moral and spiritual perfection.

For moral and spiritual perfection can only be pursued by finite men through a series of choices, in which every moment is a new beginning; and the freedom which makes those choices possible is itself a condition without which the moral and spiritual ends would be meaningless. If this were not so, if such ends could be achieved without the continuing exercise of freedom, then moral and spiritual perfection could be taught by rote and enforced by discipline— and every man of good will would be a saint. Freedom is therefore an integral aspect of the highest end. It is also, to be sure, an integral aspect of the lowest end, of total rejection of good and truth. If this is paradoxical, it is the paradox of the human condition. But paradox or no paradox, it remains true that freedom is not subordinate to moral and spiritual ends; rather it is concomitant with them, for without freedom no moral end can be achieved by the particular kind of being man is. Freedom that is not used to achieve high ends does not become something else; it does not change into another entity, "license." It is simply freedom that is not used to achieve high ends, freedom badly used; but it is still freedom. A hammer when you smash your thumb with it is just as much a hammer as when you drive a nail true.

The refusal to distinguish freedom from the ends towards which the free human being ought to move, the insistence that freedom badly used is not freedom but an indefinite something called license, is repeated again and again in the literature of the New Conservatism. Russell Kirk, in an essay called "Conditions of Freedom"* skips hither and yon through the pages of intellectual history, bringing authority to bear from Greece and India, from Israel and Christendom; it is perfectly good argument for what men ought to do, but it says nothing about freedom. It only attempts by its rhetoric to convey to the reader that freedom is doing what one ought to do. Nowhere is there an attempt to consider freedom as choice, and to come to grips with the problems of the "conditions of freedom" that arise if freedom is so understood. Freedom in this sense, the only sense in which it retains meaning, is dismissed with a quotation from Milton at his most polemical and most personally

---

* Russell Kirk, *Beyond the Dreams of Avarice* (Chicago: Henry Regnery Co., 1956), pp. 166-172.

aggrieved, a quotation from an outburst entitled "On the Detraction which followed upon my writing certain Treatises":

> This is got by casting pearls to hogs,
> That bawl for *freedom* in their senseless mood,
> And still revolt when truth would set them free.
> License they mean when they cry *liberty;*
> For who loves that, must first be wise and good.

The same Milton, however, when he wrote soberly and seriously on this question in the *Areopagitica*, magnificently vindicated the thesis that freedom to choose is the very essence of the pursuit of virtue:

> It was from out the rind of one apple tasted, that the knowledge of good and evil as two twins cleaving together leaped forth into the World. And perhaps this is that doom which Adam fell into of knowing good and evil, that is to say of knowing good by evil. As therefore the state of man now is; what wisdom can there be to choose, what continence to forbear without the knowledge of evil? He that can apprehend and consider vice with all her baits and seeming pleasures, and yet abstain, and yet distinguish, and yet prefer that which is truly better, he is the true wayfaring Christian. I cannot praise a fugitive and cloistered virtue, unexercised and unbreathed, that never sallies out and sees her adversary, but slinks out of the race,

where that immortal garland is to be run for, not without dust and heat. Assuredly we bring not innocence into the world, we bring impurity much rather: that which purifies us is trial, and trial is by what is contrary.*

This is the Milton of the great epic poems of freedom and its uses, good and evil, not the peevish polemicist of sectarian struggle. It is the Milton who celebrates freedom, understanding that for an innocent being, or for a perfect one, virtue is so natural that choice is without meaning, but that for a human being, it is choice and its freedom that is the prime condition of virtue: "As therefore the state of man now is; what wisdom can there be to choose, what continence to forbear without knowledge of evil? . . . that which purifies us [that is, brings us to virtue] is trial, and trial is by what is contrary."

But Mr. Kirk's entire essay bears with all its weight in the opposite direction. Freedom is again and again confused with virtuous ends: "submission to the will of God"; "the absence of desire"; reconciliation "with the demands of social cooperation." Implicitly and explicitly, under the guise of a discussion of freedom, it is a plea for virtue, neglecting utterly the essence of freedom.

---

* *Milton's Prose*, selected and edited by Malcolm W. Wallace (London: Oxford University Press, [The World's Classics No. 293], 1925), p. 290.

The recalcitrance of freedom

It is simple enough to come forth with a solution of the dilemma of freedom and virtue if freedom of choice as the condition of achieving virtue is ignored, and if freedom is reduced to acceptance of that which is right.

The trouble is that freedom is more recalcitrant. It is the condition of virtue, but it is also the condition of vice. It is not true, as Russell Kirk says, that "the true freedom of the person . . . subsists in community"*; it subsists in the individual. He may find freedom in communal participation, or he may find it in ignoring community, even in revolt against community. It all depends upon the circumstances; but what does not depend upon the circumstances is the necessity of freedom. Freedom can and may be in accord with social order; it can and may be in discord. There is no pre-established harmony; it all hangs upon the character of the social order.

The problem of political theory and political practice is to bring about such conditions of order as make possible the greatest exercise of freedom by the individual. But that problem cannot be solved so long as the potential opposition between freedom and virtue is passed over and freedom is defined in terms that

* "Ethical Labor," *Beyond the Dreams of Avarice*, p. 99.

ignore its essence and verbally remove the possibility of opposition.

In the "progressive" cant of the past few decades, the confusion inherent in this view of freedom has been expressed in the phrase, "not freedom *from*, but freedom *for*." The "freedom from" here deprecated is freedom in its true meaning. The "freedom for" is not freedom at all, but simply a set of ends conceived as the proper purpose of freedom. While the ends posited in this argument differ profoundly from those propounded by the New Conservatives ("freedom for" being usually conceived in terms of jobs, security and the rest of the materialist Bill of Claims), this attitude reflects the same conceptual rejection of integral freedom. Neither the welfare-statist with his materialist ends nor the New Conservative with his spiritual ends is willing to accept freedom. The word, however, is a good word, a "God-term" in Richard Weaver's terminology; and both make play with it. But neither is willing to face the conclusion that acceptance of freedom in its true meaning would force upon him: that freedom does not lead inexorably and of itself to the ends which either of them espouses, but only makes it possible for each individual person to choose between them.

In pressing the credentials of freedom, I am not maintaining that these two sets of ends are equally valid. Far from it. I regard the moral and spiritual virtues as—by all rational, prescriptive, and intuitive evidence—demonstrably the true end of man. I regard the materialist positivist Utopia to be *as an end* a lure to man's degradation (however useful material well-being is when held in due proportion). But the issue in the analysis of freedom is not the validity of the respective ends of the two parties, but their common denial that man can reach a worthy end only if he is free to reject it, that "that which purifies us is trial, and trial is by what is contrary."

Clinton Rossiter in his *Conservatism in America*, discussing the problems of liberty and security in modern society, hopes that "the new conservatism" may give us a "firmer grasp of the relationship" between them; riding over the problems that exist if liberty—freedom—is seriously considered, he says:

> Orators of the Right will continue to make capital out of the false polarity between these two most powerful of man's desires . . .*

In the manner I have been analyzing, he proceeds to reduce the meaning of liberty to that which achieves the ends he posits under the shibboleth-word, "security." He at least does it quite openly:

---

* Clinton Rossiter, *Conservatism in America* (New York: Alfred A. Knopf, 1955), p. 257.

The conservative should give us a definition of liberty that is positive and all-embracing, not negative and narrow. In the new conservative dictionary, *liberty* will be defined with the help of words like *opportunity, creativity, productivity, and security*.*

Whatever one may think of these ends (and despite their noble sound, some of them as generalizations conceal rather extensive mine-fields); even if it could be admitted that as ends they are unexceptionable and representative of the highest good—they still in no way help to define liberty or freedom. Freedom could be as well, or as badly, defined by substituting *rugged individualism* or *hierarchy* for *opportunity*, *love* or *duty* for *creativity*, *asceticism* for *productivity*, *adventure* for *security*. One could indeed continue to ring an indefinite number of changes on this note—as many as the ends which men have chosen and the interpretations they have given to these ends. But no group of them, nor all of them taken together, can help to define freedom or liberty, certainly not to "give us a definition . . . that is positive and all-embracing, not negative and narrow." For freedom is *not* "all-embracing." It is a specific aspect of the condition of man; it is neutral to ends—and presumably, therefore, "narrow"; and it is as "negative" as it is "positive," since its exercise demands that it reject all alternatives but the one it chooses.

---

* p. 258, italics in original.

One can sympathize with the effort on the part of political theorists to reduce the meaning of freedom and equate it with the ends the reductionist accepts as virtue. To do so eliminates a stubborn problem: the resolution of the dilemma of freedom and virtue, the resolution of the contradiction between man's nature as a radically free being and the exigencies of that necessary political order without which neither freedom nor virtue could long flourish. But the dilemma thus resolved is illegitimately resolved. It can be resolved, as I hope to demonstrate, but not by eliminating freedom, for freedom is essential to the being of man.

IV

WHAT KIND OF ORDER?

"ORDER" is the battle-cry of those who deny that freedom is the aspect of the nature of men which political institutions exist to serve. "Order," they insist, not freedom, is the primary reason for the existence of those institutions, the first criterion by which they should be judged. Now, of course, there can be no denial that men can live as men only in some relationship with other men; and that the sum of all the relations between men will make up some form of order. The form may vary from a quasi-anarchy to the most iron of authoritarian regimes, but some form it will have. So far, those who preach the importance of the concept of "order" in political theory are right; but so far what they stress is no more than a truism.

The key word is "some." Some order there will be

always. What is important is not order as order, but what kind of order. The task of political theory is to develop the criteria by which differing political orders can be judged in the light of principle. The mere fact that to exist man must live under *some* political order cannot be itself the standard by which the character of an order may be judged. The problem rather is *what* political order, in the circumstances of any given place and era, will best conduce to the establishment and preservation of conditions most favorable to the pursuit of the ends of man's existence.

The New Conservative differs from the collectivist liberal as to the nature of these ends. He rejects the contemporary orthodoxy which is based upon the idea that man is but a tool-bearing gregarious animal whose end is material welfare; in the tradition of the West, he posits as the end of man the pursuit of virtue. Where he fails to differentiate himself, however, from those he opposes, is in his acceptance of the idea that ends are implicit in the flux of experience. Whether that flux be thought of as materialist or Providential, and whether therefore the ends it dictates are material or ideal, both notions lead to the denial of the possibility of choice and freedom. And from this denial arises the concept of a political order where power rests of right in the hands of those who understand the true ends of existence, of those who can force men to be, in the one case, materially happy, in the other case, virtuous.

Freedom is reduced to understanding what the Fates decree; while all men understand, some men understand more than others; and those who understand the most must force those who understand less to understand more. We are back with Rousseau: "men must be forced to be free." But, as I have tried to demonstrate, men are made in such a way that they can make no ends their own except through free choice. Men cannot be forced to be free, nor can they even be forced to be virtuous. To a certain extent, it is true, they can be forced to act as though they were virtuous. But virtue is the fruit of well-used freedom. And no act to the degree that it is coerced can partake of virtue—or of vice.

Thus there remains a problem, and a very real one for the political theorist. If virtue is the true end of man's existence; if it can only be achieved in freedom; and if freedom by its nature can lead to vice as well as to virtue: what, then, of the criterion of the political order? There is undoubtedly a dilemma posed. The contradiction in the condition of man—that he can only achieve the good if he is free to reject it—has its reflection in the political sphere. The political enforcement of the good is only possible if the freedom which men must have to seek the good is destroyed.

Approaches to the dilemma of freedom and virtue

In discussing this problem, the general approach of political theory, since its beginnings in Plato, has not been essentially different from the one I have been analyzing, the approach which the New Conservatives share with the collectivist liberals. Freedom has been subordinated to the ends designated as good by the theorist, and the criterion of the good society and the good political order has been its consonance with those ends.

Doubts have arisen about this cavalier treatment of freedom, but in the main line of political thought little attention has been paid to them until, within the last 200 years, a school of thought arose that reversed the evasion of the contradiction to substitute another evasion, placing the freedom of the individual not simply as the criterion of political order, but as the sole good and end of existence. Radically secularist in its philosophical assumptions and positivist in its negation of absolute value, it turned "freedom is freedom to do the right" into "make men free and they will do the right," the right being implicitly defined as what free men will do. This solution of the problem, which is approximately that which Bentham and the two Mills held in common with so many of the political thinkers of the century they epitomized, also evades rather than faces the contradiction. The ends of human existence can no more, with respect for reality, be subordinated to freedom than freedom to those ends.

Resolution of the dilemma

Is there, then, no solution? Must we either accept the reality of freedom and deny objective value, or accept objective value and deny the reality of freedom? I would maintain not only that there is a solution but that it has been approximated in practice in a number of political societies, and most closely by the United States in the original conception of its Founding Fathers. I would also maintain that theoretically that solution has been touched on again and again,* although rarely, except in the American Constitutional debates, has it been developed as the central concept of a political theory.

The dilemma is one which can only be solved by the classical logical device of grasping it by both horns. For the difficulty is that both its major premises are true: on the one hand, freedom *is* essential to the nature of man and neutral to virtue and vice; on the other hand, good ends *are* good ends, and it *is* the duty of man to pursue them. I deny only that in the real

---

* In America, for example, by Madison and Calhoun, in England by Acton and Percy, to mention only one or two. Even in the Greek world, Aristotle occasionally approaches the solution, although his basic position is far from it.

situation with which we are dealing these two true premises are contradictories. Rather they are axioms true of different though interconnected realms of existence. How can true ends be established elsewhere than in the intellectual, the moral, the spiritual order? Where can the conditions for freedom be established but in the social order, which means—since this is where determining force centers—in the political order? A good society is possible only when both these conditions are met: when the social and political order guarantees a state of affairs in which men can freely choose; and when the intellectual and moral leaders, the "creative minority," have the understanding and imagination to maintain the prestige of tradition and reason, and thus to sustain the intellectual and moral order throughout society.

To the degree that either of these conditions is lacking, a society will not be a good society, and the individual men who constitute it will suffer in their humanity. Granted the highest development of freedom in the political order, a failure of the responsible interpreters of the intellectual, moral, and spiritual order would make freedom a useless toy by depriving men of standards by which to guide their lives. On the other hand, given the most elevated intellectual, moral and spiritual understanding, the subordination of the political order to the enforcement of that understanding, the denial to men of the freedom to accept it or reject it, would make virtue meaningless and truth rote.

There exist, therefore, two problems; but only one of them, the problem of the conditions of a good political order, is the concern of political theory in the strict sense, and therefore the direct subject of this book. There are of course interpenetrations between the spheres, effects upon each sphere from developments in the other. The very concept of freedom as the essential condition of the development of human beings depends upon propositions drawn from the intellectual and spiritual order. Deformations in the political order make the preservation, growth and propagation of fundamental truth extremely difficult. But they still remain separate realms, and the criteria of the two orders are very different.

Political theory and practice, therefore, must be judged by criteria proper to the political order; and the decisive criterion of any political order is the degree to which it establishes conditions of freedom. On the political and social level this is primary. Much could be said about the causes and remedies of the intellectual and spiritual *malaise* of our time, but that is the subject matter of another book; here I shall be able only to touch upon it briefly in a later chapter.

Rights and duties

Once this necessary separation of spheres is understood, it becomes clear what is wrong with the cardinal objection the New Conservatives bring against a politics of freedom: the argument that the rights of individuals are not unalienable, that they must be subordinated to the performance of duties. If the relation of rights and duties as a political problem is considered under the criteria of the political sphere, the falsity of this doctrine becomes apparent. The individual person lives in a social milieu constituted of other persons and groupings of persons who make up social and political institutions. However much awe and reverence may rightly or wrongly become associated with these institutions, they cannot *as such* have any moral claims upon him. Only insofar as they represent the moral claims of other persons, that is, only secondarily, does he have duties to them. The Great Commandment, which is the cornerstone of the structure of Western moral thought, reflects this hierarchy of values, ignoring utterly everything but God and individual persons: "Thou shalt love the Lord thy God with all thy heart, and with all thy soul, and with all thy strength, and with all thy mind; and thy neighbour as thyself."

If particular social institutions, which are composed of more or less determinable groups of persons, are secondary and their claims derivative, then even less can "society," which is simply an abstraction of the sum total of all the relations between persons, be a primary source of obligation in moral and political thought. When the New Conservative insists with

Burke on the claims of "this mysterious incorporation of the human race," one of two things follows. Either he must actually believe that Society is a living organism, endowed with a soul and constituting a third term that should be added to the Great Commandment; or he is talking nonsense.

Only if he is willing to take the former position, is it possible logically to defend as an axiom of political theory the proposition: no rights without corresponding duties. This doctrine, much older of course than the New Conservatism, has taken many forms; but in all its forms, as in New Conservative thought, it depends upon the belief that society or the state is a being, almost a person, who in reciprocal relationship with individual persons hands out rights as they fulfill their duties to it. In such a scheme of things, "rights" would obviously be dependent upon duties performed; but they would not be rights, they would be privileges. The rights of human beings, however, are not the gift of some Leviathan; they are inherently derived from the nature of men. The duties of human beings are not tribute owed to Leviathan; they are moral imperatives grounded in objective value. Each is independent of the other; it is not a matter of *quid pro quo*.

Rights are moral claims which each individual person has upon other persons, and upon all associations of other persons, including in particular the state; and they remain valid whether he is a good man or an evil man, whether he performs his duties or fails to perform them. Duties are obligations morally binding on each person, whatever his situation, whether other men, groups of men or the state respect his rights or trample upon them. No man can give as an excuse for failure to carry out a duty that others have failed to respect his rights. No man, no group of men, no state, can give as an excuse for depriving an individual person of his inherent rights that he has failed to perform a duty. Duties and rights both derive from the same source, the moral ground of man's nature. But if they are made directly dependent one upon the other, they cease to be rights or duties. Losing their moral autonomy, rights become privileges dispensed to the individual by society or the state, and duties become obediences extorted by power as a payment for privileges.

The *form* that the duties incumbent upon any individual person will take will depend, first, upon the position in life and the endowments of the person concerned, and secondly upon social circumstances; but the essential content of his duties, always reflecting the moral law, remains the same, whatever his position and capability, whatever the customs of society or the laws of the state. Similarly, the forms in which a man's rights are expressed may vary with time and place and custom, but the content remains the same—the right to live uncoerced by force or fraud in the possession of life, liberty and property.

The inherent nature of the rights and duties of an individual person, in short, is such that they are not dependent one upon the other. Nor, in any sense, are rights derived from society or the state, or subordinated to duties towards society or the state.

A problem, however, remains—one that can never be finally solved, although the entire structure of the social order, and first of all, the political order, the state, exists primarily as a means to its solution. That problem arises out of the dilemma of virtue and freedom, and out of the corollary contradiction that one man's freedom can be used to inhibit another man's freedom. The refusal by some persons to accept their duties, to obey the moral law, means that the rights of others have no protection from these predators unless they are restrained by force—that is to say, unless *their* freedom is interfered with and *their* rights limited. But since no man is perfect and no one can be depended upon absolutely to fulfill the whole duty of man in letter and spirit, prudential considerations require what the pure philosophical concept of rights cannot brook: that the absolute ideal of the rights of the person must be and will be modified in actual historical existence to the degree necessary to reach the closest possible approximation to that ideal for each individual person.

To say this is not to say that the inherent rights of the human being are—as ideal and as the standard by which actual practice is to be judged—any the less absolute. Nor is it to say that rights are in their essence expedient means towards "social harmony" or the reward dispensed by society or the state for duties fulfilled. Rights, rather, are obligations upon the state to respect the inherent nature of individual human beings and to guarantee to them conditions in which they can live as human beings, that is, in which they can exercise the freedom which is their innate essence. The paradox that to achieve this it is necessary in practice to restrain the freedom of individuals to interfere with other individuals, is the reason for the state's existence. And the political order is to be judged, therefore, in terms of its success in dealing with this paradox of social existence, in terms of its preservation of the conditions of freedom.

Political order and practical politics

To give primacy to principle over experience and to insist that freedom is the first criterion of the political order, is neither to ignore experience nor to forget that a complex of factors in the minds and lives of men affects the ways in which it is possible at any given time and place to achieve political conditions for the exercise of freedom. Freedom remains the criterion, principle the guide; but the application of principle to circumstances demands a prudential art. The intricate fibres of tradition and civilization, carried in the minds of men from generation to generation, always affect the realization of any general principle. Furthermore, no practical situation can be the direct reflection of a single principle, however important. The compelling, if secondary claims of other principles, though not decisive to judgment in the political sphere in the way that freedom is, do nevertheless bear upon every concrete political problem. Considering the condition of man as an imperfect being, there are likely to be a number of political orders which are more or less tolerable in terms of freedom (but none of which is perfect), as there are undoubtedly some which are intolerable.

At this point, once again one runs afoul of both the liberal collectivists and the New Conservatives. To the one, such an approach, with its concern for prudence and tradition, is unscientific in the extreme, smelling of obscurantism and the dark unenlightenment of the peasant. To the other, the emphasis on reason and principle is the arch heresy of all Jacobins and liberals, which leads directly to totalitarianism.

The collectivist liberal has no use for anything that is not operationally purposeful. One of his few inheritances from the 19th-century liberal is the engineer's approach to political and social matters. Although the 20th-century collectivist substitutes pragmatic "models" for the rational theory of the older liberal, he is just as eager to use those "models" as tools to transform the world from top to bottom to fit his scientistic preconceptions, as was his forebear to build Utopias to match his rational vision. The long-established ways of men; the multifarious modes they have found to mediate between conflicting interests and conflicting principles; the national and local peculiarities of social orders arising from the history of humankind and its great diversity: all these must be razed by the builder's demolition engines, ground to powder, to make way for new aseptic constructions that will, with maximum efficiency, cover the social landscape.

The New Conservative, on the other hand, insists, as we have seen, that the application of reason to political and social matters is dangerous in the extreme. To the degree reason is exerted at all, he demands that it be within very narrow limits and in strict subordination to the dictates of tradition. While rational reform is not ruled out for details of the social structure, the very notion of judging an existing society in its totality by rational standards is blasphemy. Prudence, therefore, becomes the master of reason, not its servant. The wisdom that counsels attention to circumstance in the application of reason becomes a blind acceptance of circumstance, which leaves the reason helpless beneath the ponderous weight of what is.

Between the Scylla of abstract application of reason

or scientific method (without prudential consideration of circumstance) and the Charybdis of unquestioning reliance on what is (which exalts expedience far above reason), the course to be steered is a difficult one. It is not only that the basic criterion of freedom must be applied to differing historical and cultural circumstances with a different perspective, since the same kind of political order which in one set of historical conditions would represent a large approach to freedom would at another time and place be close to intolerable from the point of view of freedom. Even apart from changing circumstances and varying traditions, there remains the general difficulty, existent at all times and all places, which I have already discussed: the contradiction within freedom itself, the sad fact that any man's freedom can be used, if he so wills, to restrict or destroy another man's freedom. From this there arises an ineluctable imperfection in any political theory or any set of political institutions which takes freedom as its criterion. Completely aside from the emphases or distortions that special interests—personal or group, material or ideal—may introduce, it is this contradiction which makes it impossible for any political order to reflect the pure concept of freedom with crystal clarity. Any such order must find a way whereby one man in his freedom can be restrained from interfering with the freedom of another man, a way which still maintains the protection of freedom to each man to the greatest possible degree. And in so doing, it will depart perforce from abstract purity of principle.

But to stress the impossibility of constructing a Utopia, to insist upon the inherent limitations in the nature of things that inhibit logical perfection in society, is not to resign the function of reason in political thought. Although social and political institutions can never reflect with the perfection of a geometrical image the ideal that a theory based upon the nature of man demands of them, it nevertheless remains true that it is only possible to think and act at the same time morally and intelligently in the political sphere if an ideal standard is constantly kept in view.

It is possible, of course, to act *intelligently* (for example, in a Machiavellian manner), without consideration of such a standard. It is also possible to act *morally* in the political sphere, obeying the imperatives that press upon the individual person acting in a given situation without consideration of the end towards which the political structure should be shaped —and many good and noble men have done so, following their duty where they found it. But insofar as their actions are considered *politically*, they can hardly be said to be acting *intelligently*. And certainly their thinking is not in the strict sense political thinking at all.

That the ideal can never be realized in an imperfect world is no more reason for giving up the effort to move towards it than—to use an analogy from mechanics—the impossibility of ever achieving the perfect frictionless machine is reason to give up the effort to reduce friction to a minimum. Nor, however much contemporary circumstances inhibit an easy or quick achievement of a markedly closer approximation to the ideal, is this a valid objection to the judgment of those circumstances in the light of an ideal end, to the presentation of political theory in that light, or to the demand that political activity should be considered in that light.

Objection to these conclusions can be valid only for one of two reasons. It may deny the truth of the ends posited—that is, it may differ upon the nature of men. Or it may maintain that the nature of the world in which men live is such that it inexorably demands a social and political structure of another sort, irrespective of the demands of principles derived from the nature of men. That is, it may differ upon the nature of men's relationship to their world and conceive of "social laws" as iron laws, as irrelevant to men's effort to realize their being as are the laws of physics.

But once granted that the nature of men is essentially what it has here been maintained to be, and granted that the forms of the political order can be shaped within the broad limitations of existing material circumstance by conscious effort directed towards an end, then the difficulties of achieving an approximation to that end cannot logically be adduced in objection. The kind of order a society has becomes susceptible to the criterion of political theory. Criticism of it becomes, in fact, the reason for existence of political theory and the prime duty of political theorists. The state ceases to be a mystical being to be worshipped or a set of data to be studied behavioristically; it is seen as subject to judgment by criteria drawn from theoretical enquiry, judgment which assesses it in terms of its service to the free being of individual human persons.

V

LEVIATHAN

I. View of Leviathan: *The State in Theory*

The state is not co-extensive with the totality of that which it governs; it is a definite group of men, distinct and separate from other men, a group of men possessing the monopoly of legal coercive force. And it remains thus set off, separate, whether it governs with or without the consent of the governed, with or without their participation in the choice of the governors. Even in a democratic polity, the state is not "we," identical with all the people, as is so often claimed; it is "they," those who hold state power. Rarely in political theory is the state thus presented for what it is: a special and limited institution. What is in actuality a specific power is hallowed with the aura of universality. Theory thereby gives sanction to the state's bursting the limits of its proper function —with the ever-present danger of its becoming an all-embracing Leviathan.

The state in classical political philosophy

The origin of the failure to understand that the state is a special and limited institution lies in the history of political philosophy. As a systematic discipline, our political philosophy begins with the Greeks. It is they who established its mode of enquiry and denominated the great questions with which Western political philosophy has been concerned. While in general their approach was so profound as to reach to enduring realities transcending their particular social order, the characteristics of that social order and the form of consciousness of the era necessarily precluded the concept of the state as distinguishable from the aggregate of those under its governance.

In the first place, so far as the social order is concerned, the Greek city-state, the *polis*, was a unity of political government, religious cult and community association. The opening sentence of Aristotle's *Politics* reads: "Every *polis* [state] is a kind of *koinonia* [communion, community, association] . . . It is that *koinonia* which is the highest of all and which embraces all the rest, aims at good in a higher degree than any other, and at the highest good."* This statement, like the well-known passage in Plato's *Republic*,** where, beginning the discussion of justice, Soc-

* Aristotle, Politics, I.l [1252ª].
** Plato, *The Republic*, Book II [368].

rates posits the state as the individual writ large, shows how thoroughly the concept of the state as an entity co-extensive with all citizens and with all their other associations—an entity possessing a moral being of its own—dominated classical political philosophy.

Secondly, and even more compelling to the thought of the Greeks in this respect than their practical circumstances were the limiting forms of their consciousness. The philosophical life of Greece, like the roughly contemporaneous life of Israel, had broken with the immemorial world outlook of the great early civilizations.* In these social orders civilization was first born and in them men had lived for most of their civilized existence: Egypt, Mesopotamia, China (be fore Lao-Tse and Confucius), India (before Gautama Buddha and Jainism). In these awesomely stable and revolving societies, the ultimate Truth was felt and understood in such identity with the factual presence of civil rule and social being that the judgment of social institutions by the criterion of transcendental truth was inherently impossible. Reality and symbol were so unified that God and King, Heaven and

* For the essential point here made, see the extensive and meticulous scholarly work of Eric Voegelin: *The New Science of Politics* (Chicago: University of Chicago Press, 1952); *Order and History*, Vol. I: *Israel and Revelation;* Vol. II: *The World of the Polis;* Vol. III: *Plato and Aristotle* (Baton Rouge: Louisiana State University Press, 1956, 1957, 1957). The interpretation and development of the point, however, is my own; for it he is in no way responsible.

Earth, Truth and Representation, could not in any analytical sense be separated one from another.

Greek philosophical speculation—in Hellas the parallel to the historical-existential prophecy of Israel—burst through this unity of the transcendental and the immanent, a unity in which neither word could have meaning since the universe was a cosmic unity of ultimate reality and present actuality. Between a social order below and a cosmic order above, both Greek and Jew were suddenly able to perceive an immense chasm. In their different ways, each became aware of the difference between what is and what ought to be, between the immanent play of events in the world of actuality and the transcendent source of value from which meaning and judgment are derived. But deep as this revolution in ways of thought was, it stopped short of the stark confrontation of the individual person with the ultimate source of his being. For the Greeks and the Jews political and social institutions ceased to partake, as they had done, of the essence of cosmic truth; but still they—not the individual men who made them up, but they as collectives, the *polis* or "the Chosen People,"—were the fundamental moral agents whose action might be judged by transcendent standards. There are, it is true, exceptions in the records we have. There are individuals—an Abraham at the sacrifice of Isaac, a Socrates drinking the hemlock—who for a moment stand at the center of the moral drama. But Abraham is in the end an epitome of the Chosen People; and Socrates, as he has come down to us, is the representative of the *polis* that ought to be. He has been sentimentalized as a champion of individual liberty, standing against the state. But even the most casual unprejudiced reading of the *Apology* and the *Crito*—to say nothing of the *Republic*—will show that he stood not as champion of the person, but as the prophet of the righteous *polis* against the bad *polis*. The Socrates who drank the hemlock is the same Socrates who discoursed in the *Republic;* and it is the *Republic*, in which men are but parts of an organic state, that represents the inner Hellenic feeling about the matter of political theory. The less absolute images of the political process presented in Plato's *Laws* or in Aristotle's *Politics* are imbued with the same spirit, however they may differ from the *Republic* in emphasis.

This inability to free themselves from the *polis* experienced as an organic being, of which individual men are but cells, was an omnipresent limit upon the genius of the Greeks in political-theoretical speculation. Their thought could only break outside its bounds in occasional lofty insights of the greatest of the Greek philosophers. But in their general system these forms of consciousness were never overcome. It is the measure of their genius that their analytical ability still holds our political theory in thrall, despite all that has occurred since, philosophically and theologically, to free the person from the bonds of existence as a cell in an organic state-community.

The Christian doctrine of the person

Between the Hellenic world and ours lies a second great revolution in human consciousness. The Incarnation, and the Christian doctrine of the person that flows from it, breaks finally and forever the unity of cosmos and person. The offer of Grace through the penetration of the Divine into the immanent world overcomes the lonely horror implicit in a clear and sharp separation between the world and the transcendent—a horror which had inhibited the mind from accepting such a separation and thus driven it back again and again to the cosmological fleshpots of Egypt. God's sacrifice in love bridged that gulf and made it possible for men to face each his indissoluble identity and accept its responsibilities. It now becomes clear not just that there is a dichotomy between transcendent truth and immanent actuality (the new understanding of Greece and Israel), but that only the person can be the earthly pole of the discharge between the transcendent and the immanent. The sanctity is drained out of all institutions of an earthly nature. For no community, no state, no association—only persons, individual human beings—can receive the beatific vision or be redeemed by the divine sacrifice of love.

I have said "is"—that the sanctity of institutions *is* drained out. I should have said "should be" drained out. It would be, if our theoretical thinking about political matters reached the highest level made possible by the Christian vision of the human drama. In fact, however, at this essential point—the primacy of the individual person in political thought and political practice—a portentous distortion occurs. So influenced are we by the Greek origins of our thinking about political matters that the best of our political theory remains imprisoned within their forms of consciousness. A political theory raised to the height that the Christian sense of the value of the person makes possible has not been developed.

The de-sanctification of the state is epitomized in the commandment: *Render therefore unto Caesar the things which be Caesar's, and unto God the things which be God's.* Unhappily, this has been too often understood either as an ascetic counsel to the godly man to suffer what earthly powers bring to bear upon him and to ignore the problems of civil society, or as a sanctification of the state as possessing in the area of earthly matters a divine authority. But the plain meaning would seem to be: to understand the difference between the things of God and the things of Caesar, and to think and act accordingly; neither to turn one's back upon the world, nor on the other hand to consider the political institutions that from time to time well or ill serve human needs as in any sense themselves divine.

If this precept so understood is explicitly held in mind, the primacy of the person looms so large that the secondary and derivative character of the state as a necessary, but limited, earthly institution, and not more, becomes sharply apparent. The state ceases to be seen as an institution universal and co-extensive with the sum of human relations that is called society. It becomes possible for political theory to break out of the bonds imposed on it by the men of genius who created it, to overcome the limits of the conditions of the Greek consciousness, and to attain the deeper understanding accessible to it on the basis of the Western doctrine of the person.

Utopians of Babel

These possibilities have not been realized. Political theory is still obfuscated by a fascination with the state considered as an entity to which value attaches over and above that which it derives from individual human beings. That this is so is, of course, due not only to the heritage of classical political theory.

From the beginnings of Western civilization, there have been undertones of another kind of thought, radically different from either the Classical or the

Christian, about man and his social development. Utopians, in the dream of a this-worldly paradise, unwilling to accept as an innate aspect of existence the imperfection of men, and seeing in political power the engine for the creation of a world in their own image of perfection, have glorified and divinized the state—although for different, almost for opposite reasons, than the followers of classical political theory. During the past few centuries these undertones have swelled till they have become the prevailing component of Western thought.

The origins of this outlook are obscure, but they must go back to at least the second millenium B.C. The myth of the Tower of Babel, like the historical record of the reign of the Pharaoh Akhenaton who attempted to reconstruct Egyptian society in a single generation, testifies to so early an existence of the belief that men can create a perfect world. It exists in the Hellenic world side by side with the dominant classical political theory (among, for example, the Pythagoreans and the neo-Platonists) and it persists in many of the Gnostic sects, through whom undoubtedly it was transmitted to Western civilization. Always since, it has been endemic as an underground aspect of Western thought, appearing now and again in the Utopianism and millenarianism of some medieval heresies, until it rises fully to the surface in two forms almost simultaneously: in the passionate revolutionism of Anabaptist and Puritan, and in the vision of knowledge as power, symbolized by the legend of Faust and soberly inculcated in the essays of Lord Bacon. In the colossal explosion of the French Revolution, the two forms came together. The *philosophes* of the Enlightenment are, equally with men of passion like Rousseau and St.–Just, creators of that cataclysm, and of the deification of Nation and State following from it. The dominant ideologies of the 20th century—Communism, Fascism, socialism, and that amalgam of positivism, pragmatism, and welfarism which is the ideology of the collectivist liberals—are the latest forms taken by this Utopian attitude.

Those who look on existence in this way, who conceive that the nature of men can be changed to meet the specifications of a design of earthly perfection, need perforce some mechanism through which to act. That mechanism must be one suited to the exercise of power by men who are certain that they, and they alone, understand what must be done, and who are fired by the mission to force their understanding upon the great mass of other men who do not understand. The mechanism stands ready to hand. The state, which is the sole universally accepted repository of force, need only be captured, and that force extended beyond its natural purposes.

The state, therefore, becomes the great engine of social transformation. Every revolutionary movement of the last two centuries—however much it may have begun by radical criticism of the state it found in being—ends by deifying the state it has captured and theologizing the concept of the state. Jacobinism, Marxism, Fascism, collectivist liberalism, each in its own way has joined intellectually and emotionally in the deification of the state, and each in its own way has contributed to that immense growth in the power of the state which is the effective condition of totalitarianism.

The state as mystery

From this heritage the collectivist-liberal attitude towards the state is derived. Against it classical political theory is helpless, because classical political theory shares with it an apotheosis of the state. But it is upon classical political theory that the New Conservative view of the state is founded. This is not to say that there is not an important difference between the collectivist liberals and the New Conservatives—as wide a one as there is between the Utopian and the classical theories of which they are respectively the heirs. The classical political outlook was deeply moral; its identification of state and society, and the placing of state-society as an independent entity taking precedence over the person, was the result of circumstances, a limitation of vision, not the destruction of an achieved understanding. Utopianism, on the other hand, is the deliberate rejection of an existing understanding of the nature of the person for the sake of a hubristic determination to dominate reality, to make it over in the image of the human makers.

Wide though this difference is, however, the collectivist liberal and the New Conservative are agreed in refusing to accept the state as an institution which is the expression of the power of a specific group of men, power which can only be justified in terms of a specific function. Unless the state is thus conceived, as an institution of specific function, composed of specific men in given relations, it is not only impossible to subject it to value criteria derived from the nature of the human person; it also seems to become impossible even to recognize the actuality of states as they are. It seems to become necessary to insist that they are one with the citizens they govern in a holistic unity. The simple and obvious differentiation between the governed and the governors (apparent every time an arrest is made, a tax is collected, or a judgment enforced) disappears. The state becomes "all of us," and more than any collection of each of us—an entity surcharged with value.

The development of democracy has made critical recognition of the dichotomy between the state and those whom the state governs particularly difficult. In a monarchy or an aristocracy or an oligarchy, or in such a combination of the three forms as England exhibited in the 18th century, or in that combination of aristocracy, democracy, and elective monarchy that the United States exhibited in its early days, the dogma of the state as co-extensive with the being of all the persons living under it was more easily controverted than in a social order that men think of as democratic. But the reality is fundamentally the same, whether the political order is democratic or not. Those who possess the power of the state possess it exclusively and over against the rest of society, whether their power is confirmed by hereditary right, landed property, wealth, or the democratic ballot.

In the last case, it is much more difficult to confute the fallacy which confuses the *power to pass upon who shall govern* with the *power to govern.* Even if the institutional structure of the state did not, as in fact it does, create a continuity among the holders of power, irrespective of the outcome of party politics, even if annual elections changed the governors constantly and men were forbidden to succeed themselves in power, the essential separation of the state from the rest of social existence would still remain. For the time that they were in power, the governors would still be governors. The state would still be raised out of, and exist over against, the rest of society.

To grasp this elemental distinction is the first condition of a theory of the state. If the state remains in the realm of mystery, which is proper not to institutions but to God and the final nature of men, it cannot in any serious sense be brought under theoretical consideration on a political level, for its own being is then the only possible criterion of judgment. Hegel has been much castigated in late years for his glorification of the state as the spirit of God in the world; but he only carried to a logical conclusion what our most accepted political theory implies in a more clouded way

A critical theory of the state

But if the state is regarded as an institution critically delimitable and serving a given function in the affairs of men, it can then be brought under criteria derived from higher philosophical consideration. It can be considered as all other institutions are considered. An ideal image of what it should be can be projected; given states can be judged by the criteria by which all human institutions should be judged: their adequacy in their own sphere to the achievement of the best possible circumstances in which human beings may work out their destiny. From the primary problem of politics, the tension of freedom and order, we have drawn the principles for judgment of that adequacy: those principles demand a state capable of maintaining order while at the same time guaranteeing to each person in its area of government the maximum liberty possible to him short of his interference with the liberty of other persons.

Anarchists maintain that this goal can be best achieved without any state whatsoever; and if their argument were valid, the best state would be no state at all. But, to return for a moment to a previous point in this discussion, brute facts invalidate their thesis. The nature of men and of freedom is such that some men may use their freedom to interfere with the freedom of others, to impose upon them with violence. In a stateless society, the only answer to such conduct is to return violence with violence, and this, we can be sure, would end in a Hobbesian "war of all against all." Some form of order is a human necessity. Without it, freedom itself is impossible. The state—that is, an institution recognized as the repository of legitimate violence to inhibit one man in his freedom from destroying another man's freedom—is therefore an institution called into being by the very nature of men's existence. It is a necessary and natural institution—so long as it fulfills its function and does not use its power for purposes extraneous to that function.

Furthermore, even were men not so constituted that some will always use their freedom in such a way as to interfere with the freedom of other men, even were the state not therefore necessary to protect the rights of individual persons against wrongful interference, there would still exist another problem that would make the state necessary. This is the perennial problem of the social order, the conflict of rights with rights. That conflict has always required the existence of a recognized source of justice, possessing a monopoly of rightful force by which to impose its judgment on individuals and groups of individuals. Were there no institution of judgment available to decide the conflict of rights with rights, the only recourse at the margin would be recourse to violence in the name of one right against a clashing right.

The state therefore has two natural functions, functions essential to the existence of any peaceful, ordered society: to protect the rights of citizens against violent or fraudulent assault, and to judge in conflicts of right with right. It has a further third function, which is another aspect of the first, that is, to protect its citizens from assault by foreign powers. These three functions are expressed by three powers: the police power, which protects the citizen against domestic violence; the military power, which protects the citizen against violence from abroad; and the courts of law, which judge between rights and rights, as well as sharing with the police power the protection of the citizen against domestic violence. The first two of these powers, the police and the military, coincide with the executive functions of government; the courts, with the judicial function; and the legislature enacts the laws (upon generally accepted fundamental concepts of morality) which the executive and the judiciary enforce. Insofar as the state fulfills these functions—the protection of citizens against violence, domestic and foreign, and the administration of justice, it plays a necessary role. To this degree, and within these limits, it is not possible to conceive of ordered human existence without the state. These functions must be fulfilled, and the state is defined in its essence as the institution which fulfills them.

But since this institution must possess a monopoly of legal physical force, to give to it in addition any further power is fraught with danger; that monopoly gives to the state so much power that its natural functions should be its maximum functions. Any activity not absolutely vital to the operation of the state in its functional capacity can only add further power to what is always a dangerous, if necessary, measure of power. And even that power will have to be hedged around, and divided among a number of more or less independent centers, if the state is not to become a danger to liberty. Those living under the state, to which they have yielded up the monopoly of legitimate armed force, cannot afford to yield it an iota more of control over their lives. When the state enters the economic sphere; when the state makes positive rules as to how men shall live that go beyond the preservation of the essential conditions of a free order; when the state takes upon itself the education of children or insurance against the hazards of life—with each of these steps its monopoly of force in the form of violence is fortified by control of economic, social, and ideological life. Step by step it amasses the decisive control of society. Each step makes the next one easier, and each step makes it harder to reverse the process. The state, from a natural and necessary institution in the social order, becomes a Leviathan, amassing to itself a decisive power that can only end in the destruction of the liberty of its citizens.

Not least of the conditions essential if the state is to be prevented from becoming such a Leviathan is the theoretical concept of the state that prevails. If it is a concept which is in accord with the nature of man, then the actual state will be judged by that concept and men will be impelled to act to hold the state within bounds. The image of the state projected in this book is, of course, an ideal. No historic state has ever fully reflected it, and by the nature of things it is impossible that any future state will fully do so. There is in power an impulsion to more power, which can only be limited by counter-measures. The state will always tend to move beyond its natural bounds, and the men who hold its power will always attempt to gain more power. But the need for a constant struggle to limit the state does not weaken the validity of the concept of a state limited to its natural function, as the theoretical standard by which to judge the practice and the claims of every historical state. Indeed, without such a concept, without such an ideal image, it would be impossible to combat that integral movement of power towards more power that must be combatted if freedom is to be preserved in an ordered society.

In the practical political thinking and action that go into the foundation and maintenance of a political order, the establishment of a just balance, which limits government to its legitimate functions while allowing it strength enough to carry out those functions effectively, is a most difficult problem. It requires the combination of a firm hold upon principle with a prudential understanding of the application of principle to changing and varied human situations. An extreme instance of this problem is the conflict between the demands of the state for the power to carry out its legitimate functions in time of war and the danger that such crises will create state power of a permanent kind that goes beyond those legitimate functions. Though this is an extreme instance, practical problems of the same sort, if of less urgency, arise constantly in the year-to-year life of any people. I do not mean to minimize the immense difficulties of solving them; but they can be solved, at least approximately, by a continuing process of prudential application of theoretical principles to changing circumstances.

II. Leviathan Enlarged: *The Liberal-Collectivist State*

The dominant motif of political thought today is the denial of a principled theory of politics based on philosophical consideration of the nature of man. The state is to be understood not by establishing what it ought to be and criticizing its actuality in terms of what it ought to be, but by a minute and detailed study of the functioning of states as they happen to be. And those happenings are interpreted as no more nor less than a struggle for power and gain. In the now well-worn words of Harold D. Lasswell, a Nestor of American "political science," the study of politics is the study of "who gets what, when, how."

Proponents and practitioners of this "political science," although they are united in their scorn for political *philosophy* (which, in Professor Lasswell's words, has significance only because it "justifies preferences"), strangely enough almost unanimously share a single well-defined set of axiomatic beliefs, upon which they act and which controls their "scientific" work. The human mind cannot in fact function without philosophical principles, whether they are consciously arrived at and held, or unconsciously and uncritically taken for granted. It is therefore no wonder that among contemporary liberals the relativist methodology, which denies the very existence of principles, is found in symbiosis with hard-bitten collectivist principles. These latter are not proclaimed as principles, it is true; they are simply assumed as the natural truth at which all objective investigation will arrive. Arrive, indeed, our scientists do—"value free," feverishly collecting data, "evaluating" these collections, and at the end of the process, neatly delivering the conclusions which they held to begin with. These conclusions are the credo of collectivist liberals in the political sphere, as their peculiar mixture of historical determinism with moral and methodological relativism is in the philosophical sphere.

"People," state, bureaucratic élite

Since for a century or more it has been possible to proclaim that God—and with Him the transcendental foundation of value—is dead, all value (the word is retained in decent, or in opportunist, deference to the prejudices of men) can be derived only from the facts of human existence. These facts disclose to us a world in which "the people" nominally, the state in their name, and the manipulators of "the people" in reality, control political happenings.

These three elements, the "people," the state which rules in their name, and the bureaucratic élites which in effect control the state, are the cardinal terms upon which the entire structure of contemporary liberal political science is erected. The state is the middle term by which the sanction of "the people," the ultimate authority in the liberal-collectivist cosmology, is transmitted to the élite which rules in its name. This paradigm of the social order is projected not only logically—to the degree that the atomized empiricisms of the "social-scientific method" allow of a coherent logic—but also rhetorically. The rhetorical identification of the state with the people, together with the rhetorical identification of the executive with the state and the exaltation of the expert over the political man, leads directly to the legitimization of the bureaucracy.

This bureaucracy is not composed simply of government civil servants, although it is in their hands that decisive operative power rests. It is rather a composite of several groups with different functional positions and some different parochial interests, but with an essential unity of ideological outlook and underlying interest that becomes greater year by year. It includes, in addition to the bureaucracy of the government, the opinion-molders of the mass-communications industry, the salaried manageriat,* both of industry and the trade unions—and the decisive sections of the academic personnel of the major universities, where for the past fifty years the ideology of this entire composite élite has been formed.

* "Manageriat" is, I know, a barbarous and an ugly coinage—but apt, because it reflects a barbarous and an ugly reality.

It is not accidental that the positivist-pragmatist ideology of these fifty years finds its end point in the establishment of its ideologists as a bureaucracy, backed directly and indirectly by the power of the state. The philosophical essence of the whole intellectual movement of the century has been the concept of control, of power—as surely in collectivist liberalism as in Marxism. The foundation of this kind of power in political and social affairs must necessarily be the state, whether that power is exerted directly, as under totalitarian circumstances, or indirectly, as in the circumstances of a welfarist collectivism of the type which has been steadily developing in the United States since 1932. The existence of truly independent centers of power, not subject to the state and uncorrelated by the state, forecloses success for an ideological attitude that sees its concepts as valid only as they become pragmatically operative: so many engineering principles, they have no meaning except as they are given reality in material activity. The existence of untrammeled independent centers of power in society is as frustrating to the holders of such a philosophy as the existence of untrammeled centers of direction in a building crew would be to a construction engineer. Indeed, images like this are often used by the collectivists as arguments in favor of their social and political programs. And such arguments would be compelling, if the building gang were an apt simile for the human race and if the destiny of men were, simply and exhaustively, to build, to make, to construct.

From the need to vindicate this view of man arises the other side of the liberal-collectivist position, an aspect of it which is prior both logically and in time: the relativist attack upon the image of man as an autonomous center of outgoing will. In place of that image, the relativist image is one of man as the resultant of physical and biological vectors, ascertainable and manipulable by any bright engineer. Men cease to be independent centers of will, free to act. They become either cells in a social organism whose will they reflect, or an inchoate collection of atoms that must be directed and brought into pattern as History or Progress or Science demands. The collectivist liberal and the Marxist plump for the latter alternative: men are atoms and must be organized in the proper pattern. The god who breathes through the collectivist liberal as he fulfills the mission of organization and direction is a hybrid of Science and Progress; the god who breathes through the Marxist fulfilling the same mission is a hybrid of History, Progress and Science. The alternative solution when the autonomy of men is denied—the apotheosis of Society as an organism with men as its cells—is the one towards which New Conservative thought tends; but of that, more later.

To return to the collectivist liberals: if men are

atoms to be arranged as engineering principles dictate, political power is the only force available to arrange them. It is here that the state becomes the decisive institution. It can be used directly and brutally, as in the Bolshevik revolution, or indirectly and subtly, as in the Roosevelt revolution. It is undoubtedly pleasanter to live under the conditions brought about by the latter revolution, and it is much more possible to reverse the trend; but in terms of social and political reality, the aim of the two revolutions is parallel. Each is directed towards bringing into power an élite dedicated to the principled suppression of the freedom of men as innate centers of will, in order to re-make the world in the image of its particular operational blueprint.

*The quadripartite bureaucracy**

If it should seem that I am exaggerating the significance of state power as the foundation of the position of the decisive élites, consider the actual situation. Fifty or seventy-five years ago, of the four divisions of the ruling bureaucracy, not one had any direct impact upon the lives and fortunes of the citizens of the United States.

---

* I owe to Willmoore Kendall the beginnings of my understanding of this phenomenon, to which he pointed in unpublished lectures that I have had the privilege of reading, and which I have had the opportunity of discussing with him at length in private conversation.

a. The government bureaucracy

The government bureaucracy hardly existed; insofar as government directly affected the lives of citizens (and that, except in time of war, was to a very small degree indeed), it was government as expressed in elected officials and legislatures, primarily those of the several states and municipalities. Taxes and regulations were almost entirely in the hands of the municipal subdivisions; a Whisky Rebellion in 1794 or a Pullman strike in 1894 might bring the power of the Federal government into direct contact with the citizen, but, except in time of war, this was extremely rare. The creation of the government bureaucracy as we know it today has taken place in the last few decades.

b. The trade-union and corporation bureaucracy

The salaried managerial of the great trade unions and the great corporations is almost entirely a creation of the years since 1932. Trade unions were not a power capable of impinging upon national life until they were called into existence as a major force by the Roosevelt administration, using Section 7-A of the NRA and the Wagner Labor Relations Act. The control of the corporations by a salaried manageriat that differs less and less day by day from the salaried manageriat which rules the trade unions is also a recent development. These "organization men" have succeeded to much of the power of the entrepreneurial capitalists, who have been undermined as a decisive class in the community by the taxation policies, the regulatory policies, the managed inflation and the redistributive welfare economics inaugurated by the New Deal and carried forward by every administration since, Democratic or Republican. They have no significant personal ownership of the industrial power they control, simply administering vast masses of capital in the name of stockholders, as government bureaucrats administer the state in the name of "the people." The power is theirs, but it is a form of power similar to that of the government bureaucrat or the trade-union bureaucrat; and it attracts and creates a similar human type, with similar interests and similar functions.

c. The mass-communications bureaucracy

The mass-communications bureaucracy is less directly and less obviously the creation of the state. But its immense power and decisive position would never have been achieved except for conditions traceable to the collectivist development of the state. The techniques with which that bureaucracy operates are directed towards what one of their number has called "the engineering of consent." The key word in that phrase is "engineering"; and this word implies psychological modes of persuasion directed towards the common denominator of a mass public, not the rational and rhetorical persuasion of a critical and highly individualized public. These "persuaders" had their origins in private salesmanship and "publicity," but their emergence and success as a powerful bureaucracy influencing public policy, is a comparatively new phenomenon. It only became possible with the substitution of the mass, the undifferentiated and inarticulate "people," for an independent and differentiated middle class* as the public towards which appeals on social and political questions are directed.

An independent middle class does not mean high-salaried technologists, professionals and managers, economically dependent upon conformity to the norms of the social machine. It does not mean William L. Whyte's "organization man," no matter how wealthy or how powerful he may be. It means literal independence, economic independence, for a sufficient number of persons, with fortunes ranging from what used to be called a modest competence upwards,

* John Stuart Mill thoroughly understood the decisive role of such a public, the role of the middle class in his time, in making a free social order possible. He went far astray, however, under the influence of a doctrinaire democratism, when he projected that role to the whole of the population, assuming that wholesale education could create the same qualities in tens of millions of dependent men that a select education and the influence of continuing families had created in tens of thousands of independent men.

to provide a stable center to the social order—whether this independence arises from personal ownership and management of enterprise or from income derived from land or investment. This is the public opinion which has passed judgment upon the claims of the powerful and the persuasive in all free modern societies.

The elimination of this independent, informed and critical court of final appeal, and its replacement by an undifferentiated mass subject to the emotions of the mob, has been the necessary prelude to the establishment of every despotism since the devotees of Rousseau's General Will and St.–Just's Nation, invoking the Terror against the Girondins, made the mob of Paris the arbiter of France's destinies. It is possible in the span of a generation or two to eliminate such a middle class without terror or physical liquidation. Inheritance taxes, which eat away the substance of families who concern themselves not with the accumulation of money, but with carrying forward and developing the tradition of the civilization; a steeply graduated progressive income tax, which almost entirely inhibits the possibility of establishing an estate and founding a family free from the external pressures of society: these will in the space of a few decades destroy all independence, except that of a few very wealthy families. It is this process, which we have witnessed during the past thirty years, that has largely destroyed the classes which traditionally represented decisive public opinion, replacing them with the pliable mass public of today. Harry Hopkins' "tax, tax, tax; spend, spend, spend; elect, elect, elect" is—a little expanded—an elegant syllogistic exposition of the process: tax to destroy the independent; spend to create the dependent; from the destruction of the one and the elevation of the other, maintain the power of the bureaucratic élite.

The mass-communications bureaucracy is a necessary link in this process. It could never have come into existence without the destruction of the independent position of the middle class; and its positive function is to "engineer the consent" of the engineerable, manipulable mass. It performs the function of creating agreement, which is indispensable to the well-being of the collectivist state and the composite élite which operates through it.

d. The academic bureaucracy

The academic bureaucracy—as a bureaucracy, in contradistinction to a calling, a collegium of scholars—is a creation of developing collectivism; and that act of creation has also taken place in comparatively recent years. A long history of ideological development, it is true, prepared the way for this transformation of the scholar into the bureaucrat. After the change in attitude of intellectuals that set in at the

Renaissance, signalized by Francis Bacon's words, "knowledge is power," it could only have been a matter of time before what was believed theoretically was expressed in practice. If knowledge is no longer conceived as the search for and the acceptance of truth—an occupation parallel to the occupation of the artist and the occupation of the saint—but as the acquisition of power to control and manipulate nature and man, it logically follows that an attempt will be made to realize that conception in the political sphere. The immense successes of the physical scientists in controlling and manipulating nature perhaps could be paralleled by a reconstruction of society, in which the state would play the role in transforming men that mechanical and industrial power had played in the harnessing of natural forces.

This battening urge for power on the part of the intellectuals—and in the first instance, the intellectuals of the academy who create the forms of thought of the intellectuals of every sphere in each new generation—is the efficient cause behind the revolution of the 20th century, whether its form has been Communist, socialist, "nationalist" or welfarist-liberal. It was only with the early years of this century—in the atmosphere of Progressivism and the New Freedom—that the idea that problems of statecraft and political power are in any special sense the concern of the scholar, of the professor, began to develop in this country; but once the idea took root, its effects were tremendous. It would be hard to underestimate the influence of the teaching in the great American universities, of the writing of members of the academy in such journals as *The Nation* and *The New Republic*, in preparing the way for that revolutionary transformation of the American state, the New Deal. And since the success of that revolution, men of the academy have occupied hundreds of prominent positions in the bureaucracy it produced.

The state, however, is a recalcitrant instrument for the academic planners. Power attracts men who are natively attuned to the ring of power and such men inevitably succeed in getting and keeping their hands on the levers of power. Using the academic adventurers only for their services in justifying and preparing the way for the aggrandizement of the power of the state, they realize in a rough political manner the power concepts of the collectivist theories while reducing the theoreticians themselves to the role of an auxiliary bureaucracy, well taken care of if it minds its manners, but powerless to initiate and far from the centers of control.

The natural history of this process is observable throughout the world. In the United States, where what has happened has been less dramatic (no "self criticism," no blood purges, no intellectual and cultural "lines" handed down from political heights), it has nevertheless run a similar course. In the rapturous springtime of the early Brain Trust, it seemed that the dreams of a generation of academic planners were being realized. The disillusionments with political reality of the academic participants of that day can be read in memoir after memoir—all variations on the theme of The Dream We Lost.*

The academic bureaucracy in its present form plays a significant role in the complex of bureaucracies which is given its life blood in the form of money and prestige by a Leviathan of state power that directly controls one-third of the national income and in a diffuse manner controls the general direction of social movement. But it is far from being that direct source of initiative and conscious direction, that brotherhood of engineer-philosopher kings, the vision of which stirred the heartstrings of the generation of Dewey and Veblen. The dream of a society hygienically cleansed of the "irrational," the divergent, the contingent, the merely mysterious, may well be on the way to fulfillment; but it is not being achieved, as

---

* One or two of the paladins of 1932—for example, Raymond Moley—have carried their analysis further and to fundamentals, and have reached a position critical of the entire philosophical outlook with which they set out on the adventure. But most of the witnesses show a complete unawareness of what hit them. One of the most illuminating of these memoirs—because the author retains a naive and touching personal faith in F.D.R.—is Rexford G. Tugwell's *The Democratic Roosevelt* (New York: Doubleday, 1957).

they dreamt, under their direct control. Not only has the dream failed to come true, but, in the striving for its realization, the ancient and honorable function of scholar and teacher has lost the glorious independence of a vocation dedicated to the pursuit and propagation of truth. The scholar has been reduced to a position of bureaucratic interdependence that in a happier age he would have scorned as the condition of clerks and functionaries.

This is the common fate of all ideologues who preach the virtue of massive and pervasive social power. By the creation of the immense and complex institutional forms necessary for centralized control, the projector becomes the victim of his own project. The scholar becomes the committeeman in a multi-million-dollar, foundation-financed "team" research project, or a cog in a government department; the artist, the writer, is bound to the feverish pace of the mass-communications industry. They have exchanged the independence of thought and action which is the proper activity of a free being for a minute share in the power of an immense machine.

This swallowing up of separate and individual energies in the coördinate functioning of a multiplex bureaucratic society could never have taken place without the bursting of its natural bounds by the state, as the aggrandizement of the power of the state would not have been possible without the floriation of bureaucratic social modes. And neither of these developments could have taken place without the triumph of the collectivist political theories upon which both have been based. Likewise, without their dominance, the destruction of differentiation among human beings and the creation of undifferentiated masses, "the people," (a process still not complete in the United States, although far advanced under the impact of income and inheritance taxes, inflation, public education, and the indoctrination of equalitarian dogmas), would have been impossible. That among the bureaucratized leaders of society, the major share of direct power rests with those who most clearly understand that in such a society power is an end, not a means, does not minimize the importance of the composite bureaucracy as a whole in controlling the state and manipulating the people.

Is there a liberal-collectivist theory of the state?

These three elements—the state, "the people," and the bureaucratic élite—are the constituents of the "model" (to use their own language), on the basis of which the liberal-collectivist political scientists work. It is from observation of their manipulations of these elements that their theory of the state can be deduced. It might be asked why it is necessary to deduce their theory of the state, rather than go to their writings and establish their theory directly. The fact of the matter is that, except in the writings of the openly or covertly Marxist political scientists, no explicit theory of the state can be found among them. Nor is this astonishing in view of the conditions under which political matters are studied today—conditions I have discussed in previous chapters.

The positivist and scientistic atmosphere, in which ends are exiled from consideration, precludes the study of the state, or of any institution, on a theoretical basis. Operational studies; comparative discourses upon the functioning of different states; historical discursions on the development of states; elaborate empirical collections of "behavioral" data; analyses of the functioning of power, in the spirit of Thrasymachus and Machiavelli—these are the products of the political scientists of the day, and of their colleagues, the sociologists, the social psychologists, and the non-theoretical economists, to whom what once were integral aspects of political philosophy have been farmed out. In the universities and the scholarly journals, when political philosophy is discussed, it is only by historians. The political theories of Aristotle or Rousseau or Mill, like Magdalenian stone axes, are archaeologically interesting, but one would no more think of devoting one's self to the *pursuit* of theoretical understanding than to the making of stone axes.

Still, since the universe and human beings are as they are, it is not possible to think or act without being subject to the determining forms of some theoretical position, whether it is consciously and formally recognized or not. There *is* a liberal-collectivist theory of the state, which pervades contemporary political thought and action. Because it does exist but is not put forth in explicit form, it is necessary to deduce its tenets. This needs to be done because even when it is recognized that something of a coherent theory underlies the pragmatic statements of collectivist liberalism, its theory of the state is usually equated either with the Marxist theory of the state or with that of 19th-century liberalism—depending upon the predilections of the critic. The Protean character of liberal-collectivist pronouncements can perhaps explain so opposite a pair of identifications. But both of these characterizations betray the lack of a serious effort to come to grips with the substance. There can be no doubt that similarities do exist between the liberal-collectivist theory of the state and the Marxist theory; it could not be otherwise when both are associated with collectivist theories of society and the economy. Likewise, a great many of the formal verbalisms of liberal-collectivist thought on political matters seem very close to some formulations of 19th-century individualist liberalism. Particularly when the intellectual bureaucracy, in the course of the struggle to control the state, comes into conflict with the efforts of legislative bodies to retain their Constitutional control over public policy, they assume the role of a mere accidental conglomeration of individuals oppressed by state power, which is identified, for the purpose of the drama, with the legislature. Then the liberal collectivist borrows almost verbatim the language of John Stuart Mill—as, for example, in the current discussion of the powers of investigating committees of the Congress.

Nor can it really be said, as is sometimes maintained, that the contradiction between the use of 19th-century liberal language for certain purposes and the congruence of many liberal-collectivist propositions to those of Marxism betrays an incoherent eclecticism. It is understandable how that conclusion can be reached, if one considers only the surface aspect, but nevertheless, as I shall show, there does exist a specific liberal-collectivist theory of the state.

"The General Will": justification of collectivist power

Like all 20th-century theories of the state, the liberal-collectivist theory is a variation on the Rousseauian concept of the state as the embodiment of the General Will. To understand how this concept has been able to be used in one way or another by all the revolutionists of the 20th century—Communist, Fascist, nationalist and welfarist—some peculiarities of its structure must be noted. The General Will is not the will of all, or the will of a majority, or the consensus of the interacting wills of groups and individuals, but the Will which all would have if they knew what was really good for them. Rousseau neither takes the positivist position that whatever power wants it will get, and that this is therefore right; nor, on the other hand, does he admit that there exist objective values which are in their essence right and which should therefore be the ends of political order. Rather, the theory of the General Will in a curious way combines positivist glorification of power with the appearance of a value-based justification of that power.

The pure positivist position is obvious for what it is. Its only defense against a value-based politics is power itself; and since, in the long run, even in the middle run, men inevitably seek justification for action in some end towards which it moves, a pure positivist theory of politics could never have wielded influence very far beyond the confines of the study. The theory of the General Will overcomes this practical weakness. Rousseau discarded the heritage of the Christian West and attempted to re-institute, by an act of intellectual will, the instinctive Greek identification of the good with the state regarded as a corporate body of the citizenry. What was natural to the Greeks, although it was a concept from which their best spirits strove mightily to break away, Rousseau strove mightily to re-establish as truth, against every instinct of Western civilization. Thus he became the presiding genius of the 200-year crisis of the West, in the most frenetic stage of which we live today. He could not, of course, re-institute Greek consciousness. The corporate sense of the Greeks, which made it possible for Aristotle to say that man is a political animal—an animal of the *polis*—no longer existed in a civilization which regards each individual man, not as an animal whose being rests in the state, but as a person whose being takes meaning from free personal choice of good and evil, a choice dictated by no institution.

This concept of free personal choice affects everyone in the West, even those who seem to have broken most sharply with the theological and philosophical sources from which it springs. Western man regards himself as the center of his own earthly existence. If God and transcendent value no longer serve as goals and guides in the free exercise of his choice, no corporate earthly deity can be recreated from a past civilization to play for him the ego-absorbing function that the *polis* did for the Greek spirit. His consciousness, free and without focus, retains the Western apprehension of person, but its energy, with the inner discipline of its originating world-view gone, acts destructively, like a powerful engine run amok, upon whatever crosses his path. Therefore Rousseau's attempted re-creation of the *polis* in the form of the General Will, could not recreate the classical principles of political order which had been destroyed by the attack of Machiavelli and Hobbes on value-based political theory. Rather, the concept of the deified will of the people furnished a quasi-moral justification without specific moral content, ready to be taken hold of by any "élite." Filled with whatever ideological content social circumstances and ideological predilections suggested to them, it was a tool well-adapted to be used, first to raise themselves to power, then to destroy their enemies, and finally to gain consent from the governed. These goals, particularly the last, could never have been reached under the aegis of the naked positivist glorification of power. The theory of the General Will in its various manifestations provided the necessary appearance of moral justification.

The empty abstraction whereby the General Will was identified neither with the particular will of individuals nor of groups nor even of a majority, but with an assumed underlying real will of the totality, enabled each élite in turn to fill out the lineaments of the totality whose will was holy, in such a manner that this will became what the élite wished it to be. Consent was gained and moral rectitude affirmed by an identification of the totality with those whose consent was to be secured. The *Volk* of the Nazis, the proletariat of the Communists, are but manifestations of this totality whose will is the General Will, lay figures draped out to gain the consent of the masses. These figures are presented as if they were indeed the very image of the masses, but in reality they are only representations of the will of the élite: the will of the Communist Party is the true will of the proletariat; the will of the *Fuehrer* is the true will of the German *Volk*. (This is not simple hypocrisy. The leading Communist, the leading Nazi, deeply believes that he does embody the true will of the people, as the Jacobin leaders of the Convention, Rousseau's immediate heirs, believed they embodied the true will of the French Nation.)

Once power is secured, the élite identifies itself with the state and buttresses its representation of the General Will with the prestige of the state. The state becomes the representative of the General Will; that Will always is what it ought to be; and what it ought to be is determined by the ideological certainties the revolutionist holds: Liberty, Equality, Fraternity, and the victory of the Revolutionary Nation; or the *Herrschaft* of the German *Volk;* or the dictatorship of the proletariat and the establishment of world Communism.

The liberal-collectivist theory of the state

As with the other revolutionary movements of modern times, the politics of liberal collectivism is a Rousseauian politics. It is only in terms parallel to those which are so starkly clear when we look at these other revolutionary movements that we can bring the elements—bureaucratic élite, state, "people"—which are the basic concepts of the liberal-collectivist theory of the state into a coherent whole. The connecting link, as in these parallel theories, is the General Will with all its ambiguity. But the terms of the ambiguity here are different than in Fascism or Communism; for racial *Volk* and *Fuehrer*, for Proletariat and Party, are substituted "the people" and the bureaucratic élite.

The first of these terms is very close to the first term in Rousseau's original position; the "people" as ultimate authority is a concept very similar to Rousseau's concept of the sovereign social body, whose will is the General Will. As with Rousseau, but differing from the Communists and the Nazis, there is no explicit mention of the second term. The liberal collectivist justifies political and social action as the "will of the people" and decides what the content of that will is in terms of the concepts and interests of the ruling bureaucratic élite. The function of the third term of this politics, the state, is to enforce upon people as they actually are, that is, upon individual persons, their own supposed will, that is, the program of the bureaucracy. Hallowed by the doctrine, unchallenged in a democratic society, that it represents the will of the people, the state can be utilized to consolidate the power of the bureaucratic élite which controls it.

Step by step it can move against all other centers of power towards a unified power structure.

The liberal-collectivist bureaucratic élite has little direct resemblance to the conscious unity of, say, a Communist Party. It is quadripartite, not unified. Its four parts (governmental, corporate-trade union, mass communications, and academic) are often more conscious of their differences and rivalries than of their common aims. But the identity of their underlying ideology impels them to a common front whenever and wherever basic issues are raised that would tend towards the restoration of the conditions of freedom. When they struggle among themselves, it is to gain some particular advantage for one group or another within the general bureaucratic system. Any radical challenge to the basic concepts upon which the power of the state is based, they unite instinctively to oppose with all the resources of their immense power. The state is their hope and their future. Without it their very function would disappear, and they would cease to be bureaucrats engineering their segment of the grand design to reconstruct mankind.

How, in what image, the reconstruction will proceed has become somewhat confused—there are a dozen variations on the image of the future for collectivist liberals, and this diversity of detail is what distinguishes them from conscious totalitarians; but to reconstruct, to shape, to control—this remains the constant, and it is this which seals their similarity to the totalitarian. Where God Himself created individual men free each to choose and shape his own life, the liberal collectivists, like all collectivists, like all Rousseauians, perpetrate a double *hubris:* to take God's place as creator, and to know better than God—to know that the enforcement of their design upon the individual man is a higher good for him than he could achieve by exercise of his own free choice.

This view of man and the universe could not have brought us to our present pass without the power of the state to effectuate it. Men of powerful intellect and personality might affect the consciousness of an age by their persuasiveness alone, but without command of state power they could not ride roughshod over the innate resistance of human beings to ideas that violate their essential being. Error may long persist on the basis of the intellectual skill or the charisma of its perpetrators; but without the power the state gives it to destroy opposition, its incongruity with the real nature of man will in the end defeat it. Other errors will come along, for this is integral to the process in which free human beings move towards truth. But no one of them can survive indefinitely in its distortion of reality *unless it controls the centralized power with which to drive truth underground, to prevent it from being heard.* Only one institution with such power is conceivable—the state swollen beyond its natural functions.

III. Leviathan Undiminished: *The New Conservatism and the State*

There is this much truth to John Stuart Mill's doctrine that truth will always prevail in the free market place of ideas, and this much only: given a society free of the power of a totalizing state, truth will survive alongside all the errors and will outlive each of them. Nor, given the human condition, can we expect more. Freedom, which is of the human essence, implies the possibility of producing error as well as finding truth. To achieve a good society requires men unremittingly devoted to the pursuit of good and truth; but it requires also that no one have the power to impose beliefs by force upon other men—and this whether those beliefs be false or true.

It is clear why this is so if the beliefs are false; it is more difficult to see why this is still so if they are true. Why cannot state power, if held by governors imbued with true principle, be used to force virtue upon men? Why should error not be forcibly destroyed?

The answer lies, as I hope what I have written has demonstrated, in the nature of man and of virtue. The only "virtue" that can be enforced would be a virtue that consisted in conforming one's behavior to external dictation. Truly to be able to choose good and truth requires a freedom which, unfortunately, also makes it possible for men to choose evil and error. In a word, good and truth cannot be enforced, because by their essential nature they cannot be made real in men unless they are freely chosen.

At the political level, therefore (that is, at the level which has to do with power in the social order), the essential requisite for a good society is such a division of power that no single center will be able to enforce beliefs upon men by force, or to inhibit and destroy other beliefs by force. This principle can be reduced to a simpler maxim: The state must be limited to its proper function of preserving order. But this will only be possible when the person is considered as the central moral entity, and society as but a set of relations between persons, not as an organism morally superior to persons. For if society be given a moral status superior to persons, then it follows both implicitly and logically that society has the right to create an arm to enforce its moral rights. That arm can only be the unlimited Leviathan state: if ultimate moral righteousness rests in society, it is justified in enforcing its righteousness, and the state which is its arm cannot be limited by any rights inherent in individual persons.

Pitfalls of "community"

Therefore, resistance to the growing collectivist tyranny of the century requires a theory of society and of the state that has as its first principle the vindication of the person. It is at this point—in its attitude towards the person and society—that the New Conservatism fails most signally to offer resistance to collectivist liberalism.

It is not that the New Conservatives have the urge to plan and engineer the social order; they have no stake, ideological or material, in the hegemony of the bureaucratic élite; their detestation of the values and the goals of collectivist liberalism is strong and certain; their criticism of the effects of liberal collectivism on the life of our time is penetrating and effective. No one has written with more eloquence and feeling of the horrors of a gradually collectivizing society than Russell Kirk or Robert A. Nisbet. Kirk's chapter, "The Problem of Social Boredom," in *A Program for Conservatives*,* Nisbet's chapter, "The Loss of Community," in *The Quest for Community*,** delineate the process of dehumanization of the individual human being today with admirable precision and with

* Chicago: Henry Regnery Co., 1954.
** New York: Oxford University Press, 1953.

deep concern for the oppression of personality in a collectivizing society.

Yet both of them, like the other New Conservatives, are blind to the effective cause of the conditions they describe with such justified loathing. The weight of the collective, of "society," upon the individual person, limiting his access to the transcendental sources of his being, to the foundations of value outside of history and outside of society: this is the prime cause of the human *malaise* which the New Conservatives describe so well. The "social boredom," the "alienation," which Kirk and Nisbet lament, is not the result of a "loss of community," but the result of an excess of state-enforced community. For "community" (except as it is freely created by free individual persons), community conceived as a principle of social order prior and superior to the individual person, can justify any oppression of individual persons so long as it is carried out in the name of "community," of society or of its agent, the state.

This is the principle of collectivism; and it remains the principle of collectivism even though the New Conservatives who speak of "community" would prefer a congeries of communities based upon locality, occupation, belief, caste, class, traditional ties, to the totalizing and equalizing national or international community which is the goal of the collectivists. This is to their credit. Better a multitude of enforced collectivities, so that the individual human being may wrest for himself an area of autonomy out of simultaneous partial loyalty to several of them, or out of precarious existence in the interstices between them, than a single all-embracing Leviathan community which will totally subordinate him. But what the New Conservatives will not see is that there are no solid grounds on which the kind of "community" they propose as the end towards which social existence should be ordered can be defended against the kind of "community" the collectivists propose.

Their defense may be based on taste, on preference for one kind of super-individual organism rather than another; but then there is no fundamental reason why their position should prevail over that of the collectivist. Or they could claim that the network of multitudinous "communities" which they prefer is less of a threat to the freedom of the individual person. But this argument in favor of their kind of community over the collectivists' depends upon a primary judgment that individual persons are the entities in terms of which the goodness or badness of the social order should be judged. This defense, however, the New Conservatives reject. Putting the individual person at the center of political thought is to them the greatest of political and social evils. Caught within the pattern of concepts inherited from classical political theory, they cannot free themselves from the doctrine that men find their true being only as organic parts of a social entity, from which and in terms of which their lives take value. Hence the New Conservatives cannot effectively combat the essential political error of collectivist liberalism: its elevation of corporate society, and the state which stands as the enforcing agency of corporate society, to the level of final political ends.

Apotheosis of the state

The evils around us, they see; but the underlying causes of those evils they cannot understand. Russell Kirk, for example, using so apparently innocent an example as the Federal Government's school-lunch program, can show how the liberal-collectivist bureaucracy—putatively executing "the will of the people," and on the most seemingly benevolent of motives—penetrates into hitherto local and private concerns of individual citizens. But in the next breath he will castigate the central axiom upon which a political theory that could resist such usurpations must be based.

Critical though he is of the growth of centralized state power, he insists, following Burke, that "society is an immortal being . . . a *spiritual* entity."* And, as always when the set of interrelations between indi-

* *The Conservative Mind* (Chicago: Henry Regnery Co., 1953), p. 18, emphasis in original.

vidual human beings that is social existence is raised to the level of a being endowed with corporate personality, the one error is followed logically and inevitably by another and even more dangerous one. The apotheosis of society leads directly to a theoretical concept of the state which would foreclose effective opposition to the totalizing state of contemporary society. Once it is believed that society is a being, society has rights. And by the very magnitude of its stature as compared with that of any individual person, those rights overshadow and take unlimited precedence over the rights of individual persons. A being of such grandeur that it is a veritable god, containing and expressing terrestrial existence, must have the right and the power to defend itself and to execute its will. From the deification of society arises the deification of the state, which is society in its active aspect. Believing that "society is a spiritual entity," it becomes impossible for the New Conservatives to see the state as physical power in the hands of a specific group of human beings. It becomes impossible to understand that the state, though a necessity of human existence, has an unlimited potential for evil the moment its power increases beyond the strict necessities of its function.

These disciples of Edmund Burke, however, believe with him that the state is a divine organ without whose positive action men cannot achieve virtue, that

"He Who gave our nature to be perfected by our virtue, willed also the necessary means of its perfection.—He willed therefore the state—He willed its connexion with the source and original archetype of all perfection."*

So Russell Kirk:

> Government is . . . a device of Divine wisdom to supply human wants. . . . The government may justly perform all those labors which surpass the reach of individual abilities. . . .**

It is true Mr. Kirk includes among the desirable ends of state activity, "to secure every man in his natural liberty," and this is excellent. But he adds "and to advance the culture of society," thus, by proposing for the state unnatural and swollen power, negating the end of liberty. Throughout his writing he makes it clear that, though he dislikes many of the activities of the contemporary state, he will not accept in principle its limitation to its essential functions. Insisting with Burke that society has a divine being and that from it the state derives a *mystique* independent of its limited function as an instrument of persons, he polemicizes against any political theory based upon the primacy of the individual person.

---

* Burke, *Works* [Bohn edition], Vol. II, p. 370.

** *Beyond the Dreams of Avarice*, pp. 146-147.

No doubt a state controlled by men imbued with Mr. Kirk's principles would enforce and encourage social and cultural conditions highly superior to those enforced and encouraged by contemporary collectivism, whether welfarist, socialist or Communist. Such men might even voluntarily limit the use of the power available to them through the state—though this is questionable, considering the tendency of power to corrupt and the historical record of the best of men when in command of power. But what is important on the level of political theory is not what uses men wish to make of power, but whether power theoretically unlimited (as it is bound to be if society and the state are considered as beings superior to individual persons) can possibly conduce to a good social order.

The enforcement of virtue, a persistent delusion

What the New Conservatives are saying is that the state is the proper organ for the enforcement of virtue. When this concept is combined with the antecedent concept of society as a primary moral being, the individual person's control over his destiny, his freedom to search for and to choose virtue, is absorbed into the destiny of society. Its virtue must be his virtue—which is no more nor less than the central tenet of totalitarianism.

Walter Berns, who (though he refuses to call himself a New Conservative) expresses these concepts with great ability and force, insists that "government should seek to . . . promote the virtue of citizens,"* and calls upon the classical tradition of political theory to support his argument that virtue, not freedom, is the primary principle of the state. Once again the conditions of classical society, of the society of the *polis*, are taken as the norm of human existence. The basic philosophical position of the great classical political theorists, which reflected the limitations of their vision, is elevated as the prime law of moral-political existence; their highest insights, which broke through those limitations and glimpsed the concept of the person as the center of moral existence, are forgotten. The Aristotle who wrote ". . . in order to be good one must be in a certain state when one does the several acts, i.e., one must do them as a result of choice and for the sake of the acts themselves"** is forgotten, while the Aristotle who expressed the fundamental Greek outlook, that man is primarily not an autonomous person but a *polis* animal, is taken as an oracle.

Certainly the concern of the New Conservatives with the achievement of virtue is a just concern. Ultimately this is the most important of problems. All that I am contending is that it is not a *political* problem, that it is not the concern of the state, that virtue

* *Freedom, Virtue and The First Amendment* (Baton Rouge: Louisiana State University Press, 1957), p. 256.

** *Nicomachean Ethics*, VI. 12 [1144[a]].

cannot be enforced or brought about by political means. Political thought and political action must be concerned with establishing and maintaining the conditions of freedom. True, freedom, though it is the end of political theory and political action, is not the end of men's existence. It is a condition, a decisive and integral condition, but still only a *condition* of that end, which is virtue. The New Conservatives are right when they insist that a consideration of men in society must come to grips with the problem of virtue. They are only wrong in demanding that that problem be solved by the exercise of political power. But here their error is a serious one, for it is an error which they share with the collectivists who care not at all for virtue or for freedom.

By their insistence on the use of political power for the inculcation of virtue, by their refusal to take a principled position in defense of a state limited to establishing the conditions of freedom, they disqualify themselves as effective opponents of liberal collectivism. The New Conservatives are left neither the champions of Leviathan that the collectivist liberals are, nor the enemies of Leviathan that the principled conservatives are, but mere critical observers of Leviathan undiminished.

VI

THE LOCUS OF VIRTUE

THE QUESTION may justly be asked: if the function of the state is to be limited to the establishment and protection of a free order, if the enforcement or the inculcation of virtue is beyond its rightful power, where in the social order is the authority that will guide men in virtuous paths? Before directly answering that question, it is necessary to consider some of the answers often given, answers which attempt to substitute other collective institutions for the state as enforcers of virtue. Collectivist liberalism, of course, has no answer because it cannot conceive of limitations upon the power of the state. After all, the democratic state is "we," and what "we" want is by definition virtuous—or (another variation) the just state is ruled by experts and what they decide is right. More fundamentally, however, and more honestly, most of its theoreticians would answer on a philosophical level, in their relativist and positivist mode, that the very concept of virtue is meaningless.

Enforced community

The proponents of the New Conservatism, to the degree that they are willing to accept limitations upon the power of the state in relation to virtue, fall back upon the concept of "community," and look to it as the source of moral authority in the social order. They see the danger of the aggrandizing modern state; but, although they fear its drive towards totalitarianism, they react with equal vigor against the idea of a political order grounded in the freedom of individual persons. They are arrayed as fiercely against "individualism" as they are against totalitarianism.

Russell Kirk is eloquent on this subject, to the point of denying that a man can be at once a Christian and an individualist. Robert A. Nisbet in *The Quest for Community* doggedly maintains that "individualism" and the breakdown of socially enforced community lead directly to totalitarianism. They both see Bentham, Mill and Spencer as but preparing the way for Marx, Lenin and Stalin. The line of their argument is: When men are not held together in customary communities (and "customary" in their usage means "socially enforced") they become "atomized," "alienated,"* incapable of resisting the aggrandizement of political power.

Community as here understood is not the voluntary association of individual human beings in the myriad of relationships that are available for each person to choose or to reject in a free society. Nor, in their concept of community as binding, are they limiting themselves to the necessary and inescapable associations that the conditions of existence prescribe for all men: the family, within which everyone is born and raised;** and the state without which civilized life is impossible. (I should remind my readers that, however much I have insisted upon the great potentiality of the state for evil if it goes beyond its natural bounds, nevertheless I have insisted that, limited to its natural functions, it is necessary for the proper life of men as men.) They mean, and they mean to mean, that the individual person is not the essential end of civil society.

---

* It is interesting how often this word "alienation" turns up in New Conservative writings (as it does also in the writing of "liberal" sociologists and psychologists of the stripe of Erich Fromm), when one remembers the origin of the word as used in this sense. It is the young Karl Marx's concept, at the beginning of his theoretical activity; what he presented was the drama of the separation of individual persons from a social matrix by the development of capitalism and the free society of the 19th century. His "cure" for the freedom of the individual from state and society and community, the freedom he condemns as "alienation," was . . . socialism.

** That is, outside of the constructions of Plato at his most aridly abstract, or the living nightmare of such Communist realities as the Chinese communes.

Nisbet, disturbed by the dangers of totalitarianism, champions a pluralism—but a pluralism of communities, not a pluralism of persons.

Persons as such are anathema to the New Conservative doctrine, unless they are mere symbols for orders and ranks and hierarchies, stiffly disposed as in a Byzantine mosaic, signifying the abstract virtue of diversity. But Heaven forfend that they be actually diverse, individual human beings, unranked and uncontrolled. There is no place in the New Conservative conspectus for the person as such, for those who live as individuals—"humble to God, haughty to man"—scorning the bounds of a predetermined estate, vindicating the glory of the person as person.

State or community: false dilemma

The New Conservatives present us with a false antithesis: either the all-powerful totalitarian state, grinding impersonally and brutally upon the freedom of everyone, or the subtler, quieter tyranny of "customarily" imposed community, in which no one can escape from the deadly environment of hereditarily or geographically imposed association. This antithesis is not only vicious in concept, but false in fact. It is vicious because it is directed to enlisting our repugnance to modern statism in behalf of a gentler tyranny. It is false because—difficult though the human condition is—we are not in actuality faced with the harsh dilemma of choosing between a fiercer and a milder tyranny over the human spirit.

This dilemma is not natural to the human condition; less is it derived from the central tradition of Western civilization; and still less, from the tradition of the American Republic. Those who present us with it split asunder the unity in tension by which the West has been able to preserve both the freedom of the person and the authority of truth and good, both freedom in the social order and virtue in the being of men, both the searching spirit and the authority of tradition. We are not faced with the alternative: On the one hand, a social order without values, without standards of truth and beauty and good; a philosophy unfounded on a transcendental end and an ultimate purpose; an ethos at the mercy of vulgarity and power. Or, on the other hand, a social order, Burkean in mode, constrained and controlled by the tyranny of habit, custom and prescription; a philosophy so held to precedent that it is deprived of the freedom to deepen and develop human understanding; an ethos tightly swaddled in the multitudinous wrappings of code and custom.

These, however, are the alternatives presented to us both explicitly and rhetorically by the champions of "community." Baker Brownell writes: "I doubt whether men can evaluate experience at all, or claim it, except within the integral relevance and context of the community."* Or, Martin Buber: "He alone is true to the one Present Being who knows he is bound to his place. . . ."** These concepts of the high priests of community subordinate the individual person, made secondary and derivative in value, to a whole of which he becomes but a cellular part. Although this general outlook, which permeates the writings of the New Conservatives, is more elevated in its moral ends than the materialistic subordination of man to the totalizing state that marks the social theory of the collectivist liberals (and all collectivists), it still is characterized by subordination of the person to collective entities.

No, the dilemma is a false construction. There is a third way. The history of the West has been the history of that third way, a way which has held in shimmering tension the authority of truth and the freedom of men. It has done so (sometimes less perfectly, sometimes more perfectly) by recognizing the absolute authority of truth in the intellectual and spiritual realm, while at the same time remaining aware of the contingency of institutions in the social realm and their consequent subordination to the transcendent value of the human person. It has distinguished—in

---

* Baker Brownell, *The Human Community* (New York: Harper & Bros., 1950), p. 266.

** Martin Buber, *Between Man and Man* (Boston: Beacon Press, 1955), p. 70.

turmoil and strife, it is true, but in the end it has always distinguished—between the fundamental truths that constitute the structure of man's being as a creature with a supernatural destiny, living in the natural world, and man-made certitudes, where authority can only be tyranny because truth is uncertain. Understanding this, the West has always recognized, in the representative moments of its drive towards the incarnation of its vision, that the ultimate guardians of its essential truths could not be the possessors of material authority with their power to impose their own particular version of the truth and with their susceptibility to the corruptions of power. The guardians of intellectual and moral truth, to whom the West has always given its final deference (to the destruction of those who would impose an armored truth) have been the learned, the priestly, the prophetic, skilled in the tradition—men devoted to the priority of persons over institutions, devoted not to power, but to truth and good.

Total state and "plurality of communities" do not constitute an antithesis; rather they are variants—the one, it is true, far more devastating than the other—of the same denial of the primary value, on this earth, of the individual person. The social order in tension between the authority of truth and good and the recognition of the fundamental value of the individual person—this is our heritage. It is the answer to the false antithesis of total state or all-encompassing community: a society armed against positivist nihilism and political messianism on the intellectual and moral level, and against tyranny, open or covert, on the social level.

Person, association, institution

If I inveigh against the concept of community as a decisive concept in political and social thought, or insist upon the priority of the individual person to collective groups of any sort, I am not therefore proposing a Robinson Crusoe social theory or maintaining that the person is a monad-like atom, cut off and isolated from other persons. These are the usual accusations brought by the proponents of community against the defenders of freedom. Again they propound a dilemma: either accept the priority of community to the person or stand convicted of rejecting love, friendship, all mutual action and communion among human beings. But this time, too, the dilemma is unreal; indeed, in this case it turns upon its framers. Only the independence and autonomy of the person makes love or any other valid relationship between persons possible; were human beings but parts of a larger whole, their love, all their reachings out one to another, would be but the cellular interactions dictated by the tropisms of the larger organism.

But we know from every ounce of our experience that this is not so. When we love, when we think or act mutually, when we create associations or institutions, each of us knows that this is *his* act, *his* reaching out voluntarily, to establish concert with other human beings; when we worship, each of us knows that it is *his* reaching out to the Person that is God. The dilemma is false: only individual persons, conscious each in his own uniqueness, can reach out and establish relations with other persons, relations charged with the content, vibrant with the tone, that all of us know unmistakably on the basis of our direct awareness. To assert the freedom and independence of the individual person implies no denial of the value of mutuality, of association and common action between persons. It only denies the value of coerced association.

When men are free, they will of course form among themselves a multitude of associations to fulfill common purposes when common purposes exist. The potential relationships between one man and other men are multifarious; but they are relationships between independent, conscious, self-acting beings. They are not the interactions of cells of a larger organism. When they are voluntary, freely chosen to fulfill the mutual needs of independent beings, they are fruitful and indeed essential. But they are essential only in that *some* kind of relationship to other men is essential to the nature of man. They are, as it were, essential as a *genus*—a general class of thing that human beings need; no specific imposed association as such is essential. Each man will find, as a free being, the relationships congenial to his specific needs.

The family

To this completely voluntary character of associations proper to the free nature of men, there are only two exceptions—the state and the family. Neither can be voluntary because of the human condition itself. The reasons why the one, the state, is essential (however dangerous its improper aggrandizement may be) I have discussed. But it is, as I have tried to prove, irrelevant to the question posed in this chapter—the locus of the guidance of men towards virtue—because its proper concern is not the inculcation of virtue but the preservation of an order conducive to freedom. The family is the condition into which children are born and under which they develop as human beings. As far as they are concerned, it is not voluntary—but (*pace* the worship of the child that has sprung up in the 20th-century world) neither are children as yet persons in the full sense of the word; in any social order where firm values are respected, they are potential persons, being moulded into true persons by the imposition upon them of the values of their tradition and their culture. As far as their parents are concerned, the family is, however, entered into voluntarily; marriage is, in a free society, originally a mutual voluntary act of two individuals—voluntary, even though any marriage worthy of that exalted name, is an unbreakable compact, and though the family, proceeding from marriage, creates morally indissoluble bonds of parental obligation.

The family is the most important form through which virtue is inculcated in children. But it is not the institution of the family as such that inculcates virtue; it is the persons who constitute the family—father and mother and other close relatives—who in actuality decide the issue of the moral and intellectual direction that children take. And this is so even if, as has become the mode today, an increasing majority of parents shrug their shoulders of this responsibility and turn their children over to the state and other institutions for ninety percent of their waking hours—to schools and a myriad of groupist organizations from Cub Scouts to Little Leagues, and to the great moral teachers of the television fraternity. By following this mode, parents, as responsible persons, deliberately act in a contra-virtuous way. It is not institutions, but their own personal conscious choice that destroys the conditions of virtue for their children. The family as an institution cannot guarantee the raising of the young in the paths of virtue, although the family is a necessary form; only individual persons, acting through the form of the family, can do so.

So it is with the other institutions and associations into which men enter. It is not some mystical quality of "community" which makes these institutions and associations conducive to the growth of virtue. They will assist or impede that great human endeavor, depending upon their form; but the positive content of the endeavor will always arise from the beliefs, the understanding, the devotion of the individual persons who associate themselves. The form of institutions has no power to make bad men good or good men bad. They can, under circumstances of the kind we have seen too much of in this unhappy century, restrict freedom and undermine the responsibility of the individual so that they become a serious impediment to the growth of virtue; but they cannot, of their own power, make men good. At their best, they can create favorable conditions—and that is all.

The economic order

Thus, a prevailing *mystique* of our era is the belief that a transformation of the economic relations into which men enter can, somehow, magically solve human problems and create virtue. The modern source of this belief is Marxism, with its quasi-religious dogmatic certainty that direction of the economy by the state will bring about a paradise on earth. But it is not in the Marxist form that this general idea has effectively penetrated our society; our collectivist liberals, shunning the sharp dogmatic mode of the Marxists, have adopted a more pragmatic approach to salvation by economic reconstruction—the prescriptions of John Maynard Keynes and the more sophisticated contemporary variants of his doctrines.

The New Conservatives are not, like the collectivist liberals, missionaries for the Keynesian system, but they fail utterly to see its dangers and they concentrate their attacks in the economic sphere upon the principled proponents of a free capitalist economy as "Benthamite individualists." They miss—as, considering their radical devaluation of freedom, they are bound to miss—the decisive virtue of a free economy: the restriction of the power of the state. Much else could be urged in its defense: it gives to the individual person, the consumer, rather than to the bureaucratic planner with state power the decision as to what should be and what should not be produced; it has been under its aegis that the enormous growth of human productivity in modern times has occurred. But these virtues are secondary to the preservation of the conditions of freedom by holding from the state the control of a large segment of human life.

Some of the champions of the free economy, it is true, tend to fall into the same error as their collectivist opponents, and to maintain that a free economy is itself a guarantee of a good and virtuous life. To the degree that this claim is put forward, the New Conservative criticism is just. A free economy can no more bring about virtue than a state-controlled economy. A free economy is, however, necessary in the modern world for the preservation of freedom, which is the condition of a virtuous society.

The issue is not, as it is often posed, whether Keynesian economics will "work." Many economic systems "work"—granted the ends towards which they are directed. Tribal economy worked. Oriental despotism worked. Capitalism works, socialism works, Communism works. But the truly important question is not whether an economic system "works," but, working, what ends it subserves. If this criterion is held in view, and the determination of human existence by material forces is rejected, economics must be subordinated to moral and political philosophy. The issue becomes not merely that a given economic system work, but that it be conducive to proper ends. To say that economics is a subordinate discipline does not mean that in its own sphere it should be censored in its methods of enquiry or in the objectivity of its conclusions. Economics is closest to an exact science of all the disciplines that study men and society. It is at the same time the farthest removed from philosophical competence, from the capacity to establish value.

Economics can neither establish nor confute the validity of a moral system or a political system. What it can do is to demonstrate what the results of alternate courses of economic action will be. The choice between these sets of results (and therefore between the economic systems which lead to them) is beyond the prerogative of economics. It is a moral and political choice.

For the defense of freedom, the decisive criterion of any economic system today is whether it gives to the state or withholds from it control of the economy. Keynesism is an alternative to Marxism as a mode of state control of the economy; and while its methods are slower than the methods of Marxism, more indirect in their application, it has proved far more successful than Marxism in aggrandizing the power of the state in countries with advanced economies. Only in industrially backward countries—or where, for example, as in Czechoslovakia, Communist physical force has prevailed—has the road to statism been the Marxist road of nationalization of the means of production. So successful has the Keynesian movement towards state control of the economy proven to be in industrially advanced countries (under the slogans of "progressive capitalism," or "the mixed economy"), that the very Socialist parties of such countries have given up their Marxism to embrace the more effective Keynesian methods. The most significant of these methods are: (1) state control of credit and of the interest rate, either directly or through a state-dominated central banking system; (2) "a somewhat comprehensive socialization of investment";* (3) "measures for the re-distribution of income,"** primarily through punitive taxation and state-induced inflation; (4) "the euthanasia of the rentier [that is, the "painless" doing away with those who have acquired capital, either through their own efforts or through inheritance] and, consequently, the euthanasia of the cumulative oppressive power of the capitalist to exploit the scarcity-value of capital"†—which, since the scarcity-value of capital cannot itself be eliminated, means that the usufructs of capital will be gradually transferred to the state.

Keynesism justifies—nay demands—an open and unconcealed use of the powers of the state to secure for the state a directing control over the economy; and its techniques, originally popularized as cures for depression, can be as readily employed to increase statist and bureaucratic power in prosperous times. John Kenneth Galbraith condescends to Keynes as old fashioned, but the measures he proposes, to bring a still larger share of the national income under the con-

* John Maynard Keynes, *The General Theory of Employment, Interest, and Money* (New York: Harcourt, Brace & Co., 1936), p. 378.

** p. 373.

† p. 376.

trol of the state, are the same measures of fiscal manipulation and punitive taxation that the influence of Keynes institutionalized in the "mixed economy." Where Keynes thought that the capitalists did not know how to invest and that bureaucrats could do it better by state manipulation, Galbraith thinks that consumers do not know how to spend and that bureaucrats can do it better for them by transferring purchasing power from "the private sector" to "the public sector," that is, from individual persons to the state.

The doctrines of Lord Keynes, and of the heirs of Lord Keynes, lead directly to the siphoning off of a large proportion of the property of individual persons into the hands of the state. By that token, the power of the state is swollen, and the power of persons to stand firmly on their own, independent of the state and of the pressure of any collective influence, is progressively weakened; free citizens steadily deteriorate into wards of the state. The Keynesian system leads insensibly to "euthanasia" of the free energy of persons—in its end it parallels the Marxist system, different though its methods are. The welfare state—that is, the state that draws into itself function after function that belongs to individual men (provision for the eventualities of sickness, unemployment, accident, variations in market conditions; the education of children; responsibility for the care of ageing members of the family: all the vicissitudes of life) is founded upon

Keynesian and neo-Keynesian doctrines. The end towards which it moves is the security of the anthill or the beehive, and the transformation of free men into a state-enforced similitude to the ants and the bees, creatures whose existence is social tropism.

The economic order dictated by Keynesian concepts, in this respect like the economic order dictated by Marxist concepts, is flatly evil, because it moves towards the destruction of personal freedom. The free capitalist economic order does not in itself and cannot in itself move towards virtue. It does not and cannot directly inculcate virtue; but it does, by foreclosing state control of the economy and guaranteeing the possibility of individual economic independence to some and free economic choice to all in an economy of high productivity, conduce to freedom for the person. Like all established sets of relationships between human beings, like all associations and institutions, an economic system cannot of itself be a source of virtue; it can only either inhibit the possibility of virtue by suppressing the freedom of men or indirectly conduce to virtue by helping to make men free.

The educational system

The economic order is, in the scale of human relationships, at something of a remove from the direct problem of the inculcation of virtue. The same principles, however, apply at every level of the relationships between men, and of the associational and institutional manifestations of those relationships. Consider the relationships into which men enter to provide for the education of the young—an area more directly related to the inculcation of virtue.

The symptoms of deterioration in our educational system, long apparent to serious observers, have become so obvious that the fact of deterioration is now a matter of public concern. Everyone, except the educational bureaucrats, whose vested interests are at stake, and those collectivist liberals to whom any attack on any state institution is impermissible (for our educational system has become in its decisive sector an arm of the state), agrees that something has gone wrong. But what? Why is it that the massive contemporary expenditure of time and energy and interest on education accumulates so little learning in the mind of the student? Why does he acquire so degraded a sense of values, so little direction towards virtue? Starkly, in the corruption of our children, we stand face to face with the truth that it is men and the ideas they hold that decide all the most important questions; that, as Richard Weaver has so eloquently shown, "ideas have consequences," and that it is the men who are imbued with these ideas—not the institutional forms through which they operate—who bring about these consequences.

The present state of American education is the direct consequence of the instrumentalist philosophy of John Dewey. Applied to the educational process and transmitted to the American educational system through an institutional network of associations, training schools and publications, instrumentalist theories have, in two generations, annihilated the education that, in one form or another, has for a thousand years formed the men who made Western civilization. This education, inherited from Hellenic civilization and transmuted by Christianity, moulded the men who developed Western civilization—moulded the framers of our Constitution, the founders of the Republic. It was based on the assumption that the function of the school and the college is to train the mind and transmit to the young the culture and tradition of the civilization, thus forming a firm foundation for virtue.

This assumption implied the acceptance of certain other assumptions of a philosophical kind: that there is such a thing as truth; that the tradition of Western civilization embodies the highest truths that, by the aid of reason and grace, men have been able to attain; that the criterion of value on this earth is innately the individual person, so that the claims of "society," "community," and state are secondary to and derived from him. It implied, also, definite social and political beliefs: that, although all men are created with certain inalienable rights, individuals vary in capacity and ability; that, therefore, to deprive the able of the opportunity to realize their ability, in the name of a leveling equalitarianism, is as great an oppression as to enslave the many for the benefit of the few. And it involved an important psychological presupposition: that education can be acquired only at the cost of work and pain.

The prescriptions which today define the practice of our educational system leave scarcely a trace of the great concepts of Western education. It is not that the training of the mind and the transmission of the truths asserted by our civilization have been forgotten; they have been deliberately and consciously eliminated. Those who have done the eliminating have made no secret of their intentions; they have branded these concepts as reactionary and obscurantist. For the instrumentalist there can be no value tradition worth transmitting; virtue as an end of human existence is a superstition left over from the Middle Ages; what is right and good and true is what serves as an instrument for adjustment to the society around one. The aim of education must be "life adjustment," and the method "life experience." The teacher must "impose" nothing. His role is not to teach the wisdom that a great civilization and a great nation have made available, but to "cooperate" with the child in gaining "acquaintance with the changing world," where "experience" and "free activity" will somehow, magically, educate him. Thus, he will grow up free of the "stifling authoritarianism" of the old education and become independent of mind and will.

But it is nonsense to assume that because the young are not firmly taught in the ways of virtue and drilled into serious habits of thought, they will spontaneously develop an educated independence of belief and thought. What will happen instead is what is happening. The teacher, free from the responsibility of teaching "abstract values" in a disciplined manner, has to fill the gap with something. Under pressure to bring about "adjustment" to the environment, he fills it with the current prejudices of his environment—and the prejudices of a contemporary educationist or a teacher trained by educationists are certain to reflect the prevailing value nihilism and political collectivism.

Furthermore, under the presuppositions upon which contemporary education functions, the very ability to think is destroyed. To learn to think requires effort and pain. There being no pressure to exert effort or to undergo pain, the mental habits of run-of-the-mill students become simply slovenly, while the tendency is for the bright ones to develop into brash youngsters in whom flashes of brilliance only emphasize the lack of intellectual depth. True, there are exceptions—hard-thinking young people, whose salvation from the smothering norm is the result of the surviving vestiges of firm and principled home influence, the providential and increasing presence of a few good teachers in our educational institutions, and, in recent years, the growing revolt among students against the whole structure of collectivist liberalism.

The decline of the American educational system to its present state is a classical demonstration of the thesis I have been affirming: that the inculcation of virtue depends not upon the institutional relations among men, but upon individual persons and the ideas they hold; and that institutions at their best can only create favorable conditions for individual men to act rightly, while, when they attain a collectivist authority, they inhibit the action of individual men for the good. The state of our educational system today is directly the result of the actions of men who have been imbued with fallacious ideas; and they alone are directly responsible. They were much facilitated in gaining decisive influence, however, by an institutional revolution that transformed the relation of education to the state. The preconditions for the triumph of Deweyism in education, and the consequent decay of education, were created by a process which set in more than a hundred years ago, long before the period of John Dewey's influence. The invasion of the field of education by tax-supported state authority—itself based on ideas of a statist nature—was the first great breach in the concept of government limited in power to the maintenance of internal and external order, the concept upon which the Republic was founded. The movement for universal, "free" (i.e., tax-supported), compulsory education begins simultaneously with the emergence in American history, in the person of Andrew Jackson, of the type Franklin D. Roosevelt brought to perfection, the demagogic "leader of the people." By the turn of the century the movement was largely successful. The decay of the quality of American education had already alarmed many eminent observers, and the foundation had been laid for the debacle of the past thirty years.

The principle that all men are equal before the law, which is essential to the moral functioning of a limited state, becomes steadily and disastrously distorted when the state engages in activities beyond its natural functions. Equality before the law—a principle based upon the innate and incommensurable value of each individual created person—is transformed into a universal equalitarianism that ludicrously insists upon the equality of all persons in all respects. Therefore, once the state steps in, the equal ability and potentiality of everyone must be assumed. All must be educated "equally" and in the same way. When, further, as a result of the intervention of the state, education falls under the control of a bureaucracy that acts upon these premises, the very idea of quality in education inevitably goes by the board. The end becomes not the development of the spirit of man, but its acclimatization to the mediocrity of the mass mind. It took a long time for these potentialities of state-controlled education to unfold, for the effect of the institutional environment to be fully felt, for good men and true ideas to be effectively inhibited. But the institutional situation was by its nature destructive of those who stood for quality and virtue, and favorable to their opposites. When John Dewey and his followers came along, the road was open. With quality, virtue and differentiation ruled out, their ideas gained an easy ascendancy.

When these considerations are adduced, the answer usually is: Be that as it may, without state intervention education of any kind would have been severely restricted to the few. So uncritically is this belief held, that it is never argued, only assumed. Yet, can there be any doubt that if the state had not intervened, there would have been as multifarious, diverse and brilliant a growth of educational opportunities, through the enterprise of private individuals and independent groups, as has taken place in other fields? Given the free action of individuals and groups—fired by beliefs and concepts as to what education should be, and moved by the spirit of charity or motivated by the hope of profit—if the false theories of Deweyism had gained influence in some institutions of a competitive educational network, its obvious inferiority would soon have put them out of business. Or, at the least, that inferiority would have restricted their patronage to those who could not recognize superiority. Competition would have made educational opportunities as common as it has made the automobile.

The entrance of the state into education, moving inevitably through quasi-monopoly towards monopoly, crushes all differentiation. Its opening of the way to levelling theories, dedicated to assuring that no unworthy son of a wealthy father shall receive an education he does not deserve, has made it certain that no one, rich or poor, can receive an education pitched above the mediocre. When the mediocre becomes the standard, as it inevitably does if differentiation is ruled out and education is judged by the degree to which it can adapt to the average, not only is quality destroyed, but with it is destroyed the very possibility of an education capable of laying the foundations for a virtuous life. For virtue does not become the end of a person's existence by "other directed" adjustment to the norm, or through the apotheosis of the "experience" of the natural, untaught, doctrineless young. Standards of virtue are the hard-won prize of millenia of civilization; and they can only be inculcated in the young by men devoted to them and skilled in their understanding of them—men who will teach with authority the traditions of the civilization and the doctrines of virtue. Teachers imbued with Deweyan and similar ideas are obviously incapable of fulfilling this responsibility; they are, in fact, hostile to the very thought of its fulfillment.

The present failure of American education to perform its function is the failure of individual persons to perform their functions. The institutional characteristics of the educational system do indeed make the advancement of the wrong kind of teacher and the suppression of the right kind easier; but, as an institution it does and can do no worse than that; just as, if it were properly established, it could do no better than encourage the advancement of teachers dedicated to the inculcation of virtue and discourage their opposites. Everything depends upon the individual persons who do the teaching, and upon the beliefs and ideas they hold. The locus of virtue in the education of the young lies in the persons who teach them. In the schools and colleges, as throughout the social order, it is individual persons who are decisive.

The locus of virtue in the social order: the individual person

The priority of the person and the derivative character of supra-personal entities, analyzed in this discussion of the economic system and the educational system, apply with equal force to all sets of relationships between men. Those relationships may be of the kind best described as institutions, or as associations, or as communities. They may be in their essential form necessary to human existence, like the state and the family. They may fulfill a function which is necessary, but which can be fulfilled in many different ways, like the economic system or the educational system. Or they may be totally voluntary, like a professional association, or a charitable guild, or a chess club. But all of them are instrumentalities only. Depending upon their structure, they can make the movement of human beings towards virtue easier or more difficult—but that is all.* The institution, the association, the community, is neither virtuous nor

---

* It is advisedly that I have omitted from this discussion what is the most important of the associations related to the inculcation of virtue: the association for the worship of God, the church. Questions are involved here that go much deeper than the political or the social; and I am not personally able, at this point in my life, to speak with certainty on these questions.

That no civilization can come into being or develop without being informed by one kind or another of relationship between the men who make it up and God, I am certain; that Christianity, which informs Western civilization, is the highest and deepest relationship to the Divine that men can attain, I am also certain; but I am not able to say that any single institutional church is the bearer of God's spirit on earth. And this makes it impossible for me to discuss the church in the terms of this book. At the very least, it is of the category of those institutions which fulfill a function that is necessary, but which can be fulfilled in a number of different ways. If, however, it should be true that a single church is the direct expression of God's love for men, then that church would be, like the state and the family, necessary in its essential form to human existence.

In either case, the association of human beings for the worship of God, the church, is, of all human associations, the most important and the most directly related to the inculcation of virtue. But still it is individual persons, in that association, who, with the sustenance of God's grace, themselves as persons are virtuous or not, inculcate virtue or fail to do so.

unvirtuous, and cannot itself inculcate virtue. Only individual persons can do this.

Individual persons cannot, of course, be virtuous or guide others to virtue by their own unaided powers. There is a moral and intellectual order, based upon the constitution of being, grasped and interpreted by generation upon generation, upon which men must draw. But the knowledge, the understanding, the belief, which that intellectual and moral order represents, has meaning only for sentient human beings, not for any supra-human collectivity—institution, association or community. Truth has meaning only for persons; beauty illumines the consciousness only of persons; virtue can be pursued only by persons.

A social order is a good social order to the degree that men live as free persons, under conditions in which virtue can be freely realized, advanced and perpetuated. Freedom has its risks, because it may not be virtue but vice that men advance; but all existence has its risks. Unless men are free to be vicious they cannot be virtuous. No community can make them virtuous. Nor can any community force upon them conditions antagonistic to virtue if the state does not, with its power, give coercive strength to community, and so long as the state, fulfilling its limited but necessary functions, protects individual persons from force and fraud by other persons and associations of persons.

The Locus of Virtue

The person is the locus of virtue. No other men, no associations of other men, can deprive him of the freedom to pursue virtue and inculcate virtue in others, if the state is maintained in its limited function, giving no sanction to the imposition of coercion by men upon men and protecting each man from coercion by his fellows.

Conclusion:

THE SHACKLING OF LEVIATHAN

BELIEF in the primacy of the person was inherent from the beginning in the vision which formed Western civilization. The complementary concept of freedom as the determining criterion of the good political and social order was, however, only partially realized, either theoretically or practically, until the foundation of the American republic and the framing of our Constitution. Here for the first time a polity was established based upon the freedom of the person as its end, and upon firm limitation of the powers of the state as the means to achieve that end.

For half a century or more the idea was clearly and firmly held, and the practice of the American republic closely approximated the idea. But a process of retrogression set in, first slowly, then faster and faster

—a process in which the decisive moments were the introduction of mass democratism by Andrew Jackson, the undermining of the sovereignty of the several states by Abraham Lincoln, and the naturalization in the United States of 20th-century collectivist principles and methods by Franklin D. Roosevelt. During the past thirty years that process has been frighteningly accelerated. A polity which represented the drive of men towards the full potentialities of their being has been defiled; that drive, more magnificent than any drive in the physical universe towards the moon, the planets or beyond, has been slowed down, cut short, reversed.

That there should set in a retreat from the vision of a truly free social order, and from the difficult and demanding endeavor to realize a polity that makes such an order possible, was perhaps to be expected. Before the advent of the Western concept of the person, men had lived for thousands of years of civilization and tens of thousands of years of pre-civilized human existence under conditions in which freedom was only an occasional and barely grasped concept, only a fugitive reality. But, however harsh the pressures of life, they lived in the deep security of the enveloping social womb. Freedom brings men rudely and directly face to face with their own personal responsibility for their own free actions. This is a shock.

Remembrance of the fleshpots of enveloping security ever tugs insidiously at the souls of free men. But where mind and will have been clear and firm, the temptation has been rejected.

It is confusion of mind and consequent debilitation of will that have brought the United States to our present condition. It is not, however, the men and women who make up the citizenry of America, the constituency of those who lead the nation, who have raised the cry for return to the fleshpots. It is and has been the leaders in the social order themselves, the possessors of intellectual and moral authority, who have blinded themselves to the truths of their heritage and rejected the moral responsibility of freedom. They have confused and bewildered those to whom it is their duty to give guidance and leadership. But the old truths, the old understanding still live in the hearts, the basic moral instincts, the fundamental beliefs of ordinary Americans. The established leaders can make them feel ashamed, ignorant, "backward," but they have not been able to eradicate their essential soundness.

The right instincts are there, the energy is there. For the shackling of Leviathan, the limitation of the state's invasion of the free domain of individual persons, those instincts await only intellectual articulation, that energy needs only organization. Here lies the challenge to resurgent conservatism in America: simultaneously to create a new intellectual and spiritual leadership, and on the basis of that leadership to move forward to the defeat of collectivist liberalism in the political sphere. Intellectually and spiritually, it has twin tasks: to come to grips with the prevailing relativist and positivist philosophy and confute it; and to vindicate the great tradition of freedom of the person, exposing collectivist theory, however attenuated and whatever its source, in all its insidious menace. Politically, it must organize the power of the consensus of Americans to bring to the helm of the state men devoted to limiting the power of the state, to freeing the energies of individual persons from bureaucratic encroachment—and to directing the rightful power of the state against the ravening drive of the armed and messianic collectivism of Communism.

The issue rests upon the question: can the new and rising conservative leadership release and guide the pent-up energies, the intuitive understanding of their heritage, the love of freedom and virtue in the hearts of the American people, before the converging forces of cloying collectivism at home and armed collectivism abroad destroy the very meaning of freedom? That issue rests, as every important human issue always rests, in the hands of individual persons. Nothing in history is determined. The decision hangs upon our understanding of the tradition of Western civilization and the American republic, our devotion to freedom and to truth, the strength of our will and of our determination to live as free and virtuous men.

INDEX

INDEX